Always
Be As HOT As The
Mistress *Would* Be

Credits:
Cover and book layout design by Costas Schuler
Editing by Sandy Schuler
Photography by Will Bucquoy

Printed in the United States of America

First Printing, 2018

Softcover: ISBN-13: 978-1-7328568-0-6
Hardcover: ISBN-13: 978-1-7328568-1-3
eBook: ISBN-13: 978-1-7328568-2-0

DanaBryant.com

Dana Bryant
501 4th Street
Santa Rosa, CA 95401

Table of Contents

Acknowledgements

Michael, my husband, I am everything I am because you loved me. My children Chelsea, Jacob and Brooke, you've been my reason to never give up. My grandchildren: I didn't think I could love more or have more capacity for joy but you light up my world up every day. To my father and to my mother who's passed, thank you for giving me the foundation of who I am today. Sandy, my editor, you brought the best out of me and made me a better writer, thank you, and Costas, too, for nudging me in the direction I needed to go. My personal coach and trainer Sarah, as always, you rock my world. My tribe of sisters…I don't even know what to say, how do I? You give me purpose beyond my wildest dreams. And how do I thank You, God, for everything You are and have done?…thank You.

Introduction

The truth is like a lion.
You don't have to defend it.
Let it loose. It will defend itself.

-St. Augustine

I'm often described as a powerhouse of a woman, confident, an epic visionary. Yet when I finally decided to write this book, I freaked out. I've had the idea for this book for years, I've coached and trained women on the principles, and I suddenly had this burning desire to put it to paper...but I felt panicked. I anxiously tried to silence the loud growl of hunger inside of me to write down all that I had learned over the years. Within just a few weeks' time, I felt quite clearly that the right time to write had arrived...but I wasn't havin' it. I resisted.

Finally, during lunch one day on our vacation, my husband looked into my eyes seriously and said, "Write the damn book. You're ready. I've got your back."

I physically withdrew. I felt like throwing up right there at Mel's Diner.

"What's wrong? This isn't like you," he pushed.

"I know, right? I don't get it either," I answered…but I was lying.

I did get it; I knew exactly what was up with me. Deep down, I was afraid of the feedback. *I was afraid of what women would say* (there, I said it. Ugh. Yuck. Ew.)

You see, I'm not really the fearful type. Not anymore, at least; it's been decades since I hung out with the terrified girl I used to be. These days I have my career in place, I've been living out my purpose and I have become a respected woman in my community. I have finally gotten enough distance from that pathetic, beaten girl I once was. I have become the inspiring, 'overcomer' kind of woman I fought so hard to be. When I thought about the repercussions of writing this book—if I wrote the *truth* about what I've learned—I'd have to expose the awful, dirty things I have done…possibly losing my 'place' among respectable women. I wanted to *distance* myself from that girl in my past. I'm the bold, conquer-the-world kind of chick now!

Feeling that insecurity again instantly brought those old voices back shouting in my head, thoughts I had silenced for years: *You're not good enough, not smart enough, not strong enough to take this on! People will find out about your past and discredit you. You're not worthy to be published. The friends you DO have will reject you for what you believe.* Oh, and here was my favorite: *you're a CHRISTIAN woman…you can NOT name your book this title!*

That Girl is Gone

An all-out mental assault was rocking my world. I started taking it out on my husband, then on my children, and suddenly I was disqualifying myself to do the very work I was called to do. Even my ten-year-old daughter asked, "Mom, you are walking around looking so insecure. What's going on? I'm getting scared for you." Every insecurity I had previously conquered came rushing back all at once. I was spinning. I was irritable. I was angry. I was ashamed. I was overeating. I was sad. I was selfish. I was quitting. I was...*no...wait...STOP. Stop Dana, STOP!*

Hey, you've been here before. I remembered what this felt like: the smell of fear, the taste of defeat, the deafening voices overlapping each other inside my head and the sense of freedom fleeing. I recognized this state all too well. Then I remembered that I had vowed to never let myself be overtaken by those feelings again. Not just for my sake, but also for all the women I serve.

I had lived half of my life enslaved to the voices of doubt, guilt and shame...and I had fought like hell to break free so I could make a difference in this world. I have made an impact on many lives. I've had the grit and guts to choose gratitude in the worst of circumstances, climb out of the darkest of pits and rise out of the dirtiest of ashes. This is what qualified me to write this book. I *knew* this. Then I remembered how I learned to ignore the lying voices and move forward afraid—that's how you beat the doubts and fears—you move through them anyway.

So I took a deep breath, counted the cost, picked up my pencil and started writing.

You, my dear reader, are worth it.

Same Kind of Different as Me

Yes, I have a past; a very dark past. I have lived on the streets, in a shelter, and in a prison cell. I have lived in a halfway house and a gorgeous home. I have lived on both sides of the tracks. I was raised a good Irish Catholic girl and came from a long line of financially successful women. I've betrayed a good man and stayed with an abusive one. I've cheated and been cheated on. I have been both liberal and conservative, at different seasons of my life. As my father says, "Dana, you could dine comfortably with the President and minister to the hardest of criminals in the darkest of places." My past has helped me become the person that can speak life into people...especially people that society has rejected (but God hasn't).

PAIN is an equalizer; suffering does not discriminate. We have all turned to something or someone to avoid feeling sorrow and anguish. I've mentored hundreds and spoken to thousands of women over the years, from many races and socioeconomic backgrounds. I've seen the smartest and most beautiful of women choose the worst kind of men that spins their lives out of control or just causes them plain misery. A broken heart doesn't care who it hurts.

You know the craziest part of it all? Right in the middle of the most gut-wrenching kind of pain, the kind where I literally wanted to die because I couldn't take one more second? I knew—and I mean I-knew-right-down-to-my-toes-kind-of-knew—that I was *meant for so much more.* Yeah, yeah. I didn't have self-esteem and I didn't feel good about myself, but somewhere deep down I knew I was a Rockstar...and I knew for damn sure I was worth more than the crap I was putting up with! That very conflict inside was the reason for the pain. I knew I deserved more.

Toxic relationships come in many forms and they destroy a person and their family no matter someone's background. I have seen the most innocent, motivated and talented of women make the worst life-altering decisions out of the temporary pain of an unhealthy relationship. (We don't manage heartache well anymore; we've stopped tapping into the wisdom of the generations before us.) I've observed women make choices about men that end up drastically changing their lives in ways they never imagined: giving up their dreams, walking away from their children, ripping their families apart and ruining their lives. *Over a man.* I've watched it happen privately and publicly. I've witnessed it kill a woman slowly and silently like an internal bleed, draining the life out of her body. I've seen enough. And I mean, ENOUGH!

We're Going In Deep

Don't let the name of this book fool you; we are going deep. We will be digging into the roots of our beliefs about ourselves, men and relationships, to make lasting changes. If you are reading this book it is because you want *more* than your current reality. Maybe you are in crisis, need healing or are smart enough to want advice about making the biggest decisions of your life—finding your life mate. We will walk through all this in these pages. I want to help you heal from your past, help you with your present, and prepare you for the future. I am here for you. I am familiar with pain. I have spent over 20 years on an intentional journey from heartache to living an abundant life experiencing the best in marriage.

This book is about hope and getting the everyday practical tools you need to turn your life around in as little time as possible. It does require some faith on your part. Faith in me, a woman you've never met and one that just told you about her ugly past.

You may even be tempted to stop reading because of what I already shared with you…but get over it, girl…you have baggage, too.

You *want* to learn from someone that has been to hell and back, anyways. Our battle wounds should be honored and valued among sisters. My scars give me the wisdom to partner alongside you. I will stick with you in any hot mess you've got and tell you the truth, no matter what. These scars and the wisdom they carry with them were my rite of passage into becoming the woman I am today. They have a purpose and a plan, and I did not come through them to hide who I am or what I've learned. Let's celebrate our hills *and* victory over our valleys, together, unashamed.

This journey also requires some faith in *yourself*—and your dreams—so stay with me. I double-dare you. No, triple-dare you! Take a chance and read on. This is not the how-to book you think you just picked up; the cover is colorful and pretty to catch your eye, but the reality is we have some real work to do. Even if your marriage seems perfect already—that's awesome! Still come along on this journey because I'm going to pose some tough questions that challenge you to look deeper at some of your beliefs…bringing changes to your marriage, making it better than you ever imagined. Warning: these truths I share will often resonate with you *while at the same time* cause inner conflict, if they disrupt what you believed thus far. The stakes may be high but it's so worth the risk I am asking you to take.

The exhilarating process of self-examination might not feel good at first. The doorway to freedom isn't the Instagram-perfect picture we want it to be. That's the problem, though. We want the instant gratification of a good life without doing the tough work that gets us there…and *sustains* it. We feel entitled to a good man and an amazing life, but freedom isn't free. We must learn how to maturely be responsible for our future.

I get it, though. We love books that tell us we're badasses. We soak up the positive affirmations telling us we can make a ton of money and have the career we always wanted. I buy those books too, that's cool, I read them, and I'm encouraged by them, too. I'm all about success and building a life of your dreams. I started a multi-million-dollar social enterprise with only $500. I AM a badass. I just don't buy into the *way* the culture says *women* should get there. Oh, I will help you become a badass—with real power and respect—and show you how to keep it. I understand a woman's desire to accomplish her goals. *We just can't do it the way we are doing it.* It doesn't work. We are trying to build the roof before we've built a good foundation. Or we are so adamant about building our careers we put love on the back burner, and wake up one morning feeling empty, unfulfilled, and lonely.

I will challenge some of your thinking. I may even make your skin crawl at times, most likely because I am resisting what the media and pop culture has taught us and what today's radical feminists are screaming at us. If you identify as a modern feminist, you might be offended...but let's hang in there together, and have those tough conversations with love and grace, because it's worth it and because I'm tired of us hurting each other. I'm willing...are you?

I mentioned I was terrified to write this book because of the feedback I was certain would head my way. As I begin to write this, that fear is gone. I dug deep and reminded myself *why* I am so passionate to write this to you in the first place. I don't care that there will be those that will oppose me, because I made a commitment a long time ago, to stand in the gap for the woman desperate to save her marriage, the young woman who is looking for love in all the wrong places, or the girl who has slept around so much that she has lost her way.

I am *so* excited about where we are headed because it will set you free in so many crazy and unimaginable ways, if you can get past the basic truths about men. Those may be hard to swallow but stay *curious*. I mean, what do you have to lose? It was tough for me, too. I didn't like it, either, when I began to examine the *evidence* and not just swallow what mainstream media was feeding me about marriage, dating, men and my feminine power. I discovered the truth by inquiring *is the self-serving propaganda delivered to me daily getting me the results I wanted as a woman?* After I failed in relationships and watched so many women struggle to find a good man or push him away when they did, I became hungry to find out *why*. My eyes began to open to the fact that the results weren't lining up and I wanted results! I want *you* to live abundantly, for your marriage to thrive and your family to *stay* together, joyfully. I want tangible, authentically positive outcomes! Not just hype or radical feminine rhetoric.

If It Were Easy, Every Woman Would Be Doing It

I have a request: that you commit to intentionally ponder the information I give you. Let it roll around inside of you. No one is watching, it's just you and me…and the book title will throw others off. For the record, I'll deliver the promise in the title. "Hot" you will be, while also liberated in the truest sense of the word. Just be willing to examine the advice I offer and sincerely put it to the test. Be honest with yourself, and—at least for the duration of this book—be willing to objectively look at the observations I make about men, comparing them to your own life experiences. Resist any impulse to resist. It's just information and it won't kill you. Let any difficult emotions rise, move through you, and then just release them. Stay curious.

We are also going to get a little vulgar at times so don't you dare get all religious on me! I will swear occasionally. I want to let my hair down with you. I am a woman of faith, yes, but I'm real and I won't be something that I'm not. I'm no "churchy preachy" type of Christian, neither am I an arrogant chick claiming I can say, act and do whatever I want, in front of anyone, at any time and call it my right to express myself. (Ew, that's gotten old).

With my girlfriends and my soul sisters I hold nothing back. As women, we don't really know how to be with each other anymore. We rarely trust each other, and we guard ourselves from intimate relationships with one another. We need to break through those barriers to reach our goal. I'm going to get all up in your business, to the innermost parts of who you are and how you got to where you are. Just imagine us in our sweats, bra-less, sitting at the kitchen table together with a cup of coffee, alternately crying our eyes out then laughing out loud together until we pee our pants. That's the type of sisterhood I'm after between us. It requires us to lay down our differences and rejoice in our similarities.

Don't give me any of that, "I don't need a man to be successful," stuff, either. I'm not buying it. It is true, you can be 'successful' without a man, but I believe you want a good man or you want to keep the one you have or you wouldn't have picked up this book, which is ok because we are not designed to be alone. Let's untangle our beliefs together. Let's be loyal friends and—for the love of God—finally get raw, real and vulnerable.

This book is not really *for* men. It's girl-code, packed with well-researched stuff *about* men. You can tell me off in your head if you get upset, heck, swear out loud at me but keep reading. I arrived at these truths because I was willing to be wrong. Be humble, be teachable…for the sake of your future, your children, and your grandchildren to come.

Here's the best news in the whole book up front—*you are in charge of your life, you are in charge of your relationships, you are worthy of a good man and I will show you how to get and keep one.* I don't give a hoot how bold that statement sounds, it's true. Who you choose to spend the rest of your life with is the single most crucial decision you will ever make, so sister, choose wisely.

Women Accept Too Little In The Beginning And Expect Too Much In The End

Go ahead, read that again. A woman accepts too little in the beginning and expects too much in the end. It applies to single women that just settle and married women that nag. We are out-of-balance and most often our approach to finding a man is backwards. We don't prepare ourselves to be married and we don't qualify our guy…and then after marriage we expect him to be what we never required of him when we met. There is hope! I have a solution. But first, we need to realize not only *how* we got here but how to *identify* a good man in the first place. You'll be surprised how I perceive men and why good men are so hard to find.

Got a good man already? Great! Let's work on *keeping* him. Want a good man? Yes, girl! Let's make sure you are *ready* to keep him once you've *got* him. No fantasy stuff and absolutely no sense of mediocrity are welcome here. We're going for over-the-top, madly-in-love-forever kind of love. Don't be surprised, because after we discover what a real man looks like, and after we have done deep soul work together, we can end up relating to our men and managing our relationship.

Self-possession. Sisterhood. Service. Sex.

These are 4 areas of our lives we must be proficient in. Once we are knowledgeable about and have learned each of these areas equally, we are ready to be in a committed relationship. We will attract the highest quality of men based on our level of mastery in each of these areas of our life. If you are married, you must still master these areas to create the life you want.

There is no way around it. If you sincerely want the kind of marriage you've always dreamed of, you must do the work. I'm going to love you through this, with the in-your-face kind of love you may not be used to. Listen sister, if you are going through hell, we have to keep going through that hell together, with help from above…and if you *learn* as we go, you won't smell like smoke on the other side. The pain of loneliness and a failing marriage is way harder than the work we have to do so just take my hand, you can do it.

A Woman Can Get A Man to Do Anything She Wants

Bold statement, right? I stand behind it 100% and it's the nuts n' bolts of this book. Let me add a qualifier: a *good* woman can get a *good* man to do anything she wants. I will use the term good man and good woman throughout the book. My definition of both is a person that is prepared and ready to be in a committed relationship with the intent to marry (and for women, proficient in the four areas I have just described).

I'm not writing to or for the person looking to 'hook up"…that's easy…anyone can do that. And by describing a good woman or good man as prepared to be married (qualified) doesn't make all other men and women 'bad' per se, they just aren't ready. So, let's get to the purpose of what this is all about: we're going for the good guy that makes your heart skip a beat when he smiles as he works hard to provide, protect and love you.

My good man of a husband, Michael, will tell you that I can get him to do anything I want. Not by manipulation, deceit or control of any kind, though, which wouldn't work on a good man anyway. Women by nature are influencers and experts in relationships and are emotionally equipped to affect the results we have always wanted—we just haven't been using our resources. Together, we are going to discover (or rediscover) our true source of feminine power, which we ultimately will use to get a man to do what we want. This will be a game-changer!

Grandma Panties

How to be as 'hot as the mistress would be' was a lesson I learned the hard way. We don't talk about the vibe of lustful energy out there—that's a genuine threat to our marriages—until it's too late, and if we do talk about it; it is from a reactive, victim mentality. I'd like to give you a proactive, do-whatever-it-takes-to-keep-a-family-together kind of action plan. And let's agree to stop pretending that 'being hot' doesn't matter…it fricken' *matters*!

Many years ago, I was in the middle of the worst marriage when my old friend Jack leaned in to me and whispered, "Are you wearing grandma panties?" This sudden, personal question stemmed from his concern and care for me. Jack was happily married to one of my best high school friends and had known me since I was 17. He had earned the right to speak into my life. I knew he loved me and hated seeing me suffer.

Nevertheless, his question shocked me. After a beat, I embarrassingly confessed, "Yes, I have 'grandma panties' on, Jack."

He sat back and gazed steadily at me with such obvious compassion, fully understanding all that implied, all that was going on with me. The look on his face and my comprehension of what that meant about my marriage hit me and I started to cry. He hugged me and whispered, "Sweetheart, always be as hot as the mistress would be."

I got divorced the following year. I was young, and the marriage was toxic. My life started to go in a downward spiral and often throughout those years, I would ponder the wisdom of Jack's words. Over time I realized the 'hot' part of what he said meant so much more than just grandma panties. (Of course, I wear comfy panties to bed now, but trust me sister, they are high cut and colorful.)

Jack taught me a lesson that I now live by; one that transformed my being as a woman and how I viewed myself and behaved. I don't worry about mistresses now, either. I pay attention to how *far* away she is, but I don't worry. I know that wanna-be-a-mistress-to-my man is out there, though…pitiful, sad and desperate for a good husband like mine. If I see her, I pray for her, I try to show her what's possible and that she is worthy of more as a woman. You know her, too. I know exactly how to spot her and I keep her far, far away from my man. I take keeping her away quite seriously.

That vibe of lust and betrayal is after my family and it is after yours too. Don't take it lightly. I'm tired of women having the power to change everything about their lives and yet ignore it. Hell, no. I won't let that destructive energy mess with my marriage or yours, either.

My husband, Michael, is crazy about me and he is passionately and faithfully in love with me. This didn't just happen by accident. I am vigilant about fighting off anything that might harm my marriage and you know what, I have peace and confidence about us while I do it. It's tough sometimes. I cry. I get frustrated. I have moments of insecurity. But girl, I know what I want, and I won't let anyone, or anything take it from me.

Let's learn how to guard our marriages, or our marriages still to come, together! Just imagine my entire tribe is with you. Trust me. We are one group of women you want on your side! We understand because our own lives have been forever changed by the principles and tools we are about to share with you. We are praying for you and we know, intimately, how hard the process can be. It will feel like surgery at times and it is—*spiritual* surgery. But let's tap into the innermost strength of our being and mold ourselves into the women we are designed to be. It's going to be a wild ride, but you can handle it!

You're strong and beautiful and I've got you sista!

Let's do this!

Chapter 1

Can We Handle The Truth?

Who Do We Think We Are?

I have some fantastic news. If you are reading this book, own a computer, and have access to the internet, you are one of the most *resourced* and *knowledgeable* women on the planet. You have opportunity. You have freedom. You have choice. Period. Could we work on more equality? Sure. Is there room for improvement in our lives as women? Absolutely. Let's just not forget what *we do have* in the meantime.

There is always room for progress, in all matters. There is always a need to be more conscientious to do what is right. We should always seek to be more aware and knowledgeable, to progress and learn. Women are in a constant state of change and we are getting better and smarter in so many ways. Yet in recent years as we have been moving forward, we have regressed psychologically in ways...especially in matters of the heart. Our struggle to be heard and for equality has been at the cost of our relationships. We are increasingly distancing ourselves from who we *were* as women to create a better future for ourselves. We are so desperate to be powerful that we are negating our very nature as women...Feminine. Beautiful. Desirable. Sensual. Emotional. We are throwing the baby out with the bathwater!

Are We Really Winning?

As women *we* are experiencing extraordinary successes in the boardroom, we are expressing our wild talent, we are unleashing our creativity, and we are proving ourselves in all manner of industry. I do not want to dismiss any of this, as I am just as passionate as you are about our successes. However, in our quest to find our womanhood we have also been losing ground. We are tearing our families apart and calling it empowerment. We are diminishing our true source of power. We are bleeding and hurting and pretending we're not.

Despite many odds against me, I am the Founder and former CEO (now Vice President) of a highly successful and rapidly growing social enterprise. I'm a public speaker, writer and a driven entrepreneur, so I'm not talking about our success in business. I'm talking about our *identity as women*. In our pursuit of women's equality we are exchanging our feminine voice for a masculine one. It is hurting us, and it is *unnecessary*. Don't believe me? Hang on, I will prove it.

Half of all marriages end in divorce and 80% of the divorces are initiated by women. 50% of female executives get divorced after their careers take off yet male executives tend to stay married. Divorce tears our families apart and devastates our children. Some argue that the trauma of a divorce has the *same effect on a child as a parental death.* (Let that one sink in.) There is an argument in today's culture that divorce does not impact a woman and her children to the degree I'm stating, but it's clearly not true—just talk to most women and children after divorce. It's devastating.

There is also a theory that divorce is high because women are no longer financially trapped in a marriage. If this were true, then we could argue that that same divorced woman, now financially free, can move on to marry a different man and *then* experience a successful marriage. *Not true.* 67% of *second* marriages fail and 74% of third marriages. It would appear the issue isn't about finances. I propose we aren't learning from our previous relationships.

Something quite simple has occurred to cause this level of relational breakdown. We stopped heeding the wisdom of the past! We turned our back on *what was working* in marriages for decades, and then got too damn arrogant to admit we might be headed in the wrong direction. To top that off we started shaking our fists at the men, blaming them, screaming 'oppression and abuse' at the top of our lungs. We arrogantly dismiss the generations before us, we stubbornly refuse to take responsibility and we aren't willing to be wrong...because *we are WOMEN, hear us roar!* Give me a break. That's not courage, that's fear. That's not wisdom, that's immaturity. I'm not taking the 'blame the man' bait.

There is hope for us. There is plenty of power available to us to make a change. We have simply misunderstood our femininity, misused it and tried to tap into a man's power instead. *We're not men.* We need to get over it.

Men Are Not The Enemy

We must shift our perception of men to truly embrace our femininity. I'm not here to debate the waves of feminism in history or truly to spend a lot of time on my opinion about modern feminism. The intent of this book is not to piss anyone off, although my candor on these matters will likely cause some controversy. It's a controversial and passionate topic so I get that there are strong opinions on the matter. I just want us to step back and look at how it *affects our relationships with men*. I will fight for our equal rights politically and in the workplace all day long, right alongside of you. I likely won't do it *the way* the modern feminists are doing it but that's my *right* as a woman, right?

Men aren't the enemy and I refuse to believe they are. We are engaging in friendly fire on our fellow humans and as a western culture we are killing off our good men. I see it every day in the media and when I listen to other women.

Men are aggressors, and we must neutralize all aggression. We must neutralize the gender roles. This message gets louder by the day. We are on an all-out assault on masculinity. The masculine traits of men (and worse, boys!) are under siege. Literally. Further, the message that women are, in general, victims of masculinity has become some sort of badge of honor among women. We don't call it that, but we sure do talk like it's true, as if it's some tie that binds us together. I have worked hard to disengage myself from this ridiculous theory. Men are not bad because of their masculinity. I propose that evil men exist because they don't have *enough* masculinity. Stay with me.

We are not oppressed *because* of these traits in men, in fact we are the better *for* them. Let's lay down our hurt and get to the bottom of this mess.

Listen, I have attended a domestic violence institute, a long-term rehab, and I've been in prison. Before you judge, I was an excellent student, outgoing in school, ambitious, well-mannered with a dream to be a lawyer someday (I had a gift for arguing. Ha!) I had many things going for me, but I couldn't appreciate the good opportunities I had because I was a brat—a spoiled little girl in an adult body.

My self-worth was in the toilet. (I never even heard of the word *self-worth*.) I had no idea what was wrong with me. I didn't understand that it was selfish expecting some amazing man to just drop into my lap. I just knew I had an image in my head of the kind of guy I dreamed of and when I didn't meet him in my teens, I started to unravel. I didn't realize I was trying to fill a hole inside of my heart with a man.

My mother tried to communicate in her own way that I was better than that, but she had a family history of verbal abuse, so she used those communication methods on me. She was only 18 when she had me, as well, so…I was rebellious for as long as I could remember. My parents were often divided on how to respond to and discipline me.

I am blessed with many natural gifts but *all I wanted was a man.* The hole in me began to grow when the man of my dreams didn't arrive. It wasn't that obvious to those around me; I hung in there by faking happiness and appearing to be ambitious and driven. It's what those around me expected. Then when I finally found a man I believed would fill the hole, he beat me and broke my heart. I stayed with him because I had no know with the cycle of abuse and I believed him every time he said he would change. In my 20's I used drugs for the first time, which led to crime, until one day I literally 'woke up emotionally' while on my way to prison for five years.

Some people have a similar version of my story. Prison doesn't always have bars. There are all kinds of prisons we put ourselves into. Some cause women to bleed slowly, never experiencing love and life to its fullest. I call these types 'dead woman walking': where they have lost all hope in their dreams and have settled for a man that never fulfills her. When she looks in the mirror, she doesn't like what she sees. If you are any version of these, I promise you there is more. So much more.

Now because of my past, I have dealt with parole officers, mental health psychiatrists, counselors, battered women experts, and suicide prevention advocates. You know what one thing they all have in common? *Every single one of these professionals told me that what happened to me was the MAN'S fault.* There was only one exception the entire way, my federal parole officer. I am still personal friends with him today, nearly 20 years later.

Even the prison counselors—*inside the very place that was making me pay a punitive price for my crimes*—let me off the hook emotionally, allowing me to blame the abusive man. Everywhere I went they discussed the aggression of men and offered some type of psychological way to blame them.

Today, at every turn, we are making men the enemy. It allows us to escape some level of responsibility in our own choices. At every turn, women are given the opportunity to be a victim. Oh, we don't like that word. You probably get quite irritated when I say it, but our culture is increasingly making a way for us to not take any responsibility for our part.

Yes, I was beaten badly. I was abused, cheated on and had my mind messed with *real* bad. For over 15 years now I have made it my mission to minister to women that were abused in every imaginable way. These women have been molested by their fathers, stabbed and shot by their boyfriends, and pimped out by men they thought would never hurt them. If anyone could make the case that 'men are horrible violent creatures and we need to neutralize their gender for the safety of women,' it would be my tribe of sisters and me. But for over 15 years we have chosen another way of dealing with the men that hurt us and it is a road rarely traveled despite the extraordinary freedom and great marriages it produces. I know probably most of you did not deal with heartache in the foolish way that I did but it doesn't matter. I am speaking to every woman: we must wake up to the sound of our own voices letting us off the hook. Our culture will let us slide and give us an excuse for our reality...*but the consequences in our lives will not.*

Don't get me wrong, I am not in any way attempting to further victimize those that have been victims. I live and breathe to protect women, but I won't do it to the point of their own detriment. You can't scream oppression with me because I fully understand the death sentence you hand to a woman when you keep her a victim. When we identify ourselves as a survivor, it's like we are these beautiful birds with one wing stuck in the fence, never able to fly.

I experience daily the tragedy of what happens to a woman when you *keep* her a victim and not allow her to take full responsibility for her actions. I know there are plenty of exceptions where women have no responsibility at all in what was done to them. Rape and violence are never ok and there is never a reason to be violated this way. But let's just keep it real: men are not the enemy and we must own our own stuff. There are bad men and there are good men and we are going to talk in detail about how to find the good ones. How can we make men the enemy while at the same time trying to find the man of our dreams and/or create the marriage we are longing for?

He Doesn't Owe You

These days we feel entitled to a good man *just for being born female*. We believe we are *owed* our Knight-in-Shining-Armor. I'm not sure if we are even conscious about it. When it's time to date, we start looking for him, that guy in our dreams. We assume he's automatically going to manifest to fulfill the fantasy in our minds' eye. Yes, we should believe we are queens and are worthy of our kings... but are we *ready*?

By age 8 we have picked out our wedding dress and the venue. We've dreamt every detail. Girl, we had the wedding, the house, and even what he looks like planned for years. However, we are losing the art of *getting ready for him*. We must prepare *ourselves*. Women are constantly told they are 'enough' now. This is true. You were always *enough*. All of us are worthy of being loved. I get the purpose of the message because we have low self-esteem among women. But 'being enough' is only *half* of the message— *we also need to be ready*—and if we don't teach readiness, we create an illusion of finding a good mate before discovering the best version of ourselves. We set ourselves up for failure.

We don't do the challenging work to be a high-value woman, but we expect him to have done what he needed to do to meet the image in our daydreams.

It's a set-up, for all involved. We wake up one day and realize we didn't marry a prince, we settled for a frog because *we attracted what we were ready for.* Trust me. When you are ready for your prince he'll arrive...because only a true prince would dare approach you. However, I believe in the sanctity of marriage and honoring the vows you have taken, so this book is *not* a license to divorce your frog! You chose him so now we have some work to do. You can't *change* him, but you can *get* him to do anything you want. (Yup, there I go again.)

The point is that yes, we are responsible for the choices we have made, and we can shift the direction we are headed. I do want you to be encouraged and hopeful but I'm also not here to tickle your ears and co-sign your fantasy. Let's build a life for you and your family, on a solid foundation, one that's not easily shaken.

Stop Lying to Yourself

In the coming pages, we are going to break down and examine the basic nature of a good man. I hope by now we can at least be open enough to discuss what we *really* want in a man, not what we might have convinced ourselves we want as a way of settling or what we tell our friends that we want to be socially accepted. Remember, what we want from a good man speaks to our own basic nature as women.

I am not a psychologist, but neither am I terribly impressed with most of them these days. I think they're half the problem. I'd rather speak to a person directly to get their perspective than trust a psychologists' viewpoint on a matter. I have many years of experience working with women, from prostitutes to power-houses. There is very little differences between us, other than a series of bad choices and a family history of chaos. I've never met a woman that didn't long for a strong and confident man. We don't crave weak and passive men; that's not attractive to us. If we look past all the crap we've been told about men, we can't lie to ourselves any more. We know what we want: a hunk who's brave and secure, a protector, a provider. We want him to be attractive to us and for us. We want him to cherish us and rescue us from harm. We want him to lead us and raise our children *with* us.

Great news. Good men *want* to be that guy. Good men *are* that guy.

When I stopped lying to myself and started preparing, I met my husband. He's hot, big, strong, tough and doesn't let anything happen to me or our children. He is a leader. He has fought when he has had to. He's the kind of guy people call when they're in trouble. He is a good man, and I prepared myself for him. *I had to.* I was tired of all the losers I was meeting. He prepared for me, as well, because he *was* a loser and decided to become a high-value man because he wanted a chick like me. It's a simple, straightforward formula, we women just make it complicated. We aren't mindful that we lie to ourselves because we want to escape the work it takes to become a high-valued person ready for a high-valued mate.

Girlfriend, the harder part is being with a loser. Compared to that, it's much easier to do the work to secure one of the good guys. Don't make it like I'm being 'judgy' over the value of humans, either. We are all valuable as human beings. Just try marrying a guy that cheats on or hits you or is so passive he doesn't provide or protect you, then come to me and tell me he is the same value as a good man like my husband. Um, *not.* They're not equal in the way we measure values, at all.

We've become so hyper-sensitive about valuing one another that we aren't holding people to a high standard anymore. We've become this nation of 'anything goes,' but the truth is, anything *doesn't* go when you get right down to it. Wake up! Look, if a woman isn't taking care of herself, let's guide her to change and encourage her self-care. We keep lowering the bar and blaming it on societal roles. Instead why don't we raise the bar, keep it high, and have something to look forward to? (This coming from a woman that *was* a total loser and who coaches men and women *out* of being losers.) Look, we *know* when we're being a loser and not living up to our potential. It's not only society's fault. People are drawn, innately, to successful, good-looking people...and I don't just mean super thin models or buff guys. Body size isn't really a factor, body confidence is. I mean, we can sense when we should be caring for ourselves more or when we aren't giving our greatest contribution to our communities. We know when we are being a loser and it's really not anyone's fault, just our own.

Pain Has Purpose

When I found myself sitting in a prison cell over trusting the wrong man, I knew I had to take full responsibility for the actions and choices I had made that got me there. My pain ran deep. For five long years I waded through the most gut-wrenching sorrow of being separated from my little girl, but I used my time wisely. It wasn't easy. To be daily facing the reality that I chose the love of a bad man over the welfare over my own child crippled me some days. Shame and regret felt like heavy chains that bound me so tightly sometimes it was hard to breathe. The ache of saying goodbye to my two-year-old was so bad at times I wanted to end my own life. I couldn'tI had been selfish enough! Frankly, I had been ridiculous enough. How could I say I loved a man that beat me and cheated on me? How, damn it? How? I knew the answers, really, I did, but it just felt better when I screamed out loud, "Why, God, why?" It made the pain ease, but the reality was so damn real, there was no way to escape the evidence of my own selfishness. *My daughter didn't have a mother because I picked a guy that had no idea how to be a man. (Shit,* that still hurts a little if I stay there too long.) Maybe others' consequences aren't as real as a prison cell, but there are countless women in chains locked in their own personal hells. Let's get them out!

Even though I was daily living in a system that allowed me to be the victim, I knew I had to make a very big decision: *would I allow my circumstances to destroy me or would I prepare myself to inspire others?* I had to *take steps* to do something different and change my life. I had to study and learn, with humility, being willing to listen to other women who knew better than I did. I had to do the hard work of exposing my fears, being willing to be wrong, and finally let go of all the defense mechanisms and attitudes I had built to protect myself. I had to catch a vision that was greater than the pain I was going through, and when I did I anchored myself to it with every ounce of my being. It's carried me through to you today...that vision of something greater is the very reason you're reading these words.

Further, I was determined to not let my tears be forgotten or wasted, damn it. My pain was going to *mean* something. I decided that what I had learned at such a high price was going to be the very thing I would teach to others. I *have* mastered the areas I will walk you through. I am far from perfect, but I am skilled, I am a warrior, and I know my power.

Your soul yearns to *live out your purpose,* too. We long to be a part of making the world a better place, to contribute to something larger than ourselves. It's what makes you feel alive, wanted, worthy, empowered—all the things you crave and desire. *All the things that happen to also attract and keep a good man.* Why are we surrendering it all to randomness? Why are we not intentionally using our pain of previous relationships as a way of guiding us? Why don't we listen to the voice of the elders in our lives that sacrificed much for the sake of staying married? We don't suffer nobly anymore.

Relationships are what matters most. They're the bonds that hold humanity together. We chase our careers, work hard to be great mothers and still have heartache when it comes to the men in our lives. Why? God made man and woman to be partners, linked together in Holy Matrimony, as one unit. It's a good plan. It is not best to be alone. I didn't make the plan, I just decided to live by it. Financial success, our challenges, our children's successes and even our purpose are, by design, meant to be a shared story *with* someone. It's a love story...a beautiful, romantic and sacred love story. We women want our love story! It's who we *are*. It is built into our bodies and our minds and our psyches...and our emotions reveal its truth.

Let's give ourselves permission for this to be true. We want our prince charming, we want to share life with him. I understand, we all do, there's nothing wrong with that dream and in no way are you less for wanting it! We are fairytale dreamers! I love that about us. It's what drives us to care for our family and make our house a home.

Let's celebrate it. Understanding the truth of what we want will lead us to get it. Let's stop diminishing and denying who we are and what we want! We *can* have it all. I can testify because I have it all. I am not talking about fantasy, here, we've done enough of that. You *can* live an awesome life 90% of the time. The other 10% is just, well, *life*.

Have a Little Faith

This is not a religious book and we will discuss faith very little. I think you can tell by now, I am not your 'average Christian', whatever the heck that means. I go to church. Church is a hospital for the sick and I *was* sick and needed to gather regularly with others because being together makes us better. Maybe you judge me because of my faith or maybe you're a Christian that thinks my style isn't religious *enough*. What I do hope you get about me by now is that I don't care about your opinion of me, but I *do* care about the impact I make, in your life as well. Beyond that, I don't give a hoot for the haters. Haters gonna hate. (If you haven't heard that expression yet, we've gotta work on getting you out more often! I'm 46. My daughters stay on me to be fresh and hip, I reach more women this way. I take my reach seriously.)

I am quite tired of the division between us women. I am exhausted with the level of attention expended towards trying to divide us. Aren't you getting pissed off at all the B.S. about our rights while we are scratching each other's eyes out? This is what I am *not* doing here.

I want to speak to your feminine voice...the one that some of us stopped listening to. I'm not into proving your political beliefs are wrong or mine right, that is getting us nowhere. We need to get back to being sisters first. We can always argue later! I know if we are fulfilled as women then we can work on the other issues together. I care about your heart, I care about your relationships, I care about your sons and daughters and your husband or husband yet-to-be. Your future *matters* to me.

The purpose of this book is also not to try to convince you if there is a God and if you need Him. There *is* a God and you *do* need Him...that's just the truth...but what you do with that truth is totally up to you. I would suggest, though, that there is evidence of God everywhere you look. I would boldly state that when you have felt alone in your despair, God was there with you. And when you need more strength than you have, He will give it to you. Your faith is weaved into the very fabric of your purpose. God gives an abundance of grace, strength and motivation to help you on your path to a new, best life, whether you believe in Him or not. He's there, cheering you on with me because He and I are cool like that. We want the same thing for you, your *freedom*.

I can promise that if you seek Him, you will find Him. I will end this subject on this—I invite you to whisper in your heart throughout this book the most powerful three words I have ever uttered: "God help me."

Always Be As Hot As The Mistress Would Be

Chapter 2

The Freedom of Knowing Why

The practical tools I will ask you to use to transform your relationships with men might seem difficult to do consistently. But hang in there, because if you have not mastered the areas I propose it will be impossible to get the maximum benefit. The humility, courage and strength required to work this plan is reserved for a good woman who is willing to pursue wisdom and isn't easily swayed by the popular opinion of those around her.

I understand how you will feel as you read this book. Until I learned I needed to love a man with complete acceptance and trust, without withdrawing it, I could NOT do what I am asking you to do, either. Until I was self-possessed (calm, confident, in control of one's feelings, composed), had a tribe of sisters for support, had a mission to serve and understood sex between a good man and a good woman, I would not have been able to see these changes through. This plan takes a mature woman who has developed her character enough to have the discipline required, especially at the beginning.

Maybe you are like I was, wondering why I had a pattern of behaviors that kept leading me to destruction and never getting me where I wanted to go, no matter how much I *tried* to change. Common advice wasn't working for me because it seemed solely aimed at 'taking care of myself' first. (Taking care of yourself is vital but it must combine with learning how to relate to others and developing our communication skills for successful relationships.) Even as I developed my character and transformed my way of being, I still found it difficult to shift or break the patterns the way I am asking you to do—until I discovered WHY. *Why men are the way they are.*

Early in our marriage, when my husband and I would have a conflict and I *tried* to respond the way I knew (by now) I needed to respond, it was like my very skin was going to burn off, I had so much resistance to it. I could barely get the words out. I was perplexed why it would be so hard to change a behavior that clearly was not getting me the results I wanted from a man.

A rebel yell would build up inside me: *I refuse to be taken advantage of. I won't let him win. If I don't argue, he will just think he can control me. I deserve to be heard. He is not going to tell ME what to do. Hell no, I'm not going to give in!*

Sound familiar?

Those were the same thoughts I had when I was with bad men in my past. Now that I had a good man, these thoughts still influenced my behavior, making it difficult to respond to conflict in new ways. I needed to become *proactive* in making my relationships *better*, instead of *reactive*, causing the drama I seemed to love to manifest. I am dramatic, almost theatrical by nature, so it spilled over heavily into my relationships. I knew I needed total transformation in my thinking, my responses and my attitudes, so the changes would be habitual and conflict would not be so difficult to get through.

I needed real answers and understanding. By the time I found those answers, I was so worn out, so plain ready to change that I just surrendered to the process, giving up my need to be right. I had never really agreed with the bitter women railing against men on TV so I wasn't totally shut down and unwilling to look at the evidence. Since I had been raised by an easygoing dad and a tough-as-nails grandfather, I was intrigued *why* I ended up picking such an abusive guy. As I had worked with so many women in broken relationships, and found myself in them too, I was obsessed with finding the answers.

Relating to men with emotional freedom and peace of mind comes when we understand *why men are the way they are.* Who are *men,* and why do they think how they think and act like they act? I've heard debates about those questions over the years. I've certainly heard plenty about how masculine men can be dangerous, even that masculinity itself is toxic, causing men to be violent, aggressive and overly ambitious. I think there is so much information about men like this that we just kind of get overloaded, go braindead, tune it out and just hit the bar, the gym or go to work hoping to find a guy that fits our dreams.

Be Strategic

Why was I so unskilled at finding a good man? It seemed much easier for other women around me (until I took a closer look). Why didn't I get the results from men that I desired and why was it so complicated and confusing? Why did the world increasingly tell me men were dumb or acted like babies and then tell me to go marry one? Why is the media telling me I am powerful and at the same time let me off the hook for being a victim of men? Why was I so attracted to a man that was masculine but so resistant to his attempts to lead me? Why was I so dead set on believing that to be in control of my life I needed to control every part of a relationship? Why weren't the countless classes, sessions with counselors, group meetings, outside mentors and women's rights advocates teaching me *why* this kept happening? Why wasn't I learning how to find and keep a good man from *real examples*, and not from a political agenda? Why was the message always I *deserved* a good man *because* I am a woman (hear me roar) and not how to *get a good man by becoming a good woman?*

And for the love of God, why did it take so long for me to ask WHY?

The Answers are in the Questions

I had to start asking myself these tough questions that no one else was. I had to be willing to lose the very identity that I had believed was protecting me, the identity that I held on so desperately to that it led me to prison. In federal court a judge once said to me, "I think a very bad thing happened to a very good girl". I held on to that statement like it was breath to my lungs. *Yes, I am a good girl and I would be amazing and successful if it just weren't for that bad man.* Most of us hang on to some version of this statement.

But the truth inside of me was fighting to be set free. No, *'a bad thing happened due to me being an unprepared girl'* was more like it. That young girl was too stubborn to listen to her mother and the generations before her because *she* knew better. That young girl was trying to act liberated with her body simply because it seemed to be the *thing to do* (freely having sex before marriage with men that were uncommitted and unqualified themselves). That young girl *never admitted* how rejected she felt when the men she slept with didn't consider her worthy enough to marry. And that young girl's life began to unravel as one guy after another did not treat her the way she had imagined in her dreams.

I went around acting like I had it together, never telling anyone the depth of pain the rejection caused me. Then when I did meet a guy that said the things I had been waiting to hear, and that first punch to my face came, I was so deep into the fantasy and so far removed from reality that I was convinced he was sorry when he said he would never do it again. Thus the cycle began. The truth was that I never even heard of 'the cycle of abuse' when I found myself *in* one 25 years ago. Only until I landed in rehab did I discover how many women had also been abused by men.

Yet, here I am stating that men are innately good and worthy to be honored. *Why?*

I could have clung on to the victim role for the rest of my life… many women do. I had been clinically diagnosed with Battered Woman Syndrome somewhere along the way, so everywhere I went there was sympathy for my pathetic life. That sympathy felt good until the years of tears began to run dry, the court case was over, and no one was left to defend me. That sympathy had felt like a warm blanket during the traumatic season when the wounds were so tender I needed a safe place to heal. But it had served out its purpose once I woke up one day to realize no one cared about my story anymore. I was only 25 years old, then, when I had to sober myself up in prison, and those days felt like my freedom was an eternity of time away. I was so young and beautiful then I can't tell you how often I was asked how could I have done what I had done.

But that journey brought me to you, and I do not define myself by who I *was*. I look back and think of those thousands of women I met along the way, whose stories were sad like mine. We are all so much alike: we get heartbroken, we get lost in the pain, and most of us have this constant nagging voice inside of our heads asking, "Why, God? Why can't I find a good man and be happy?"

I want to sit with you in the reality of what it feels like to be lonely. I want to hold you in whatever your current despair may be, if you're married or not. I want to acknowledge that we all want to be loved passionately and I want to give ourselves permission to share with one another how hurt we are when it doesn't turn out the way we wanted. Not to live in the hurt, but simply to expose the truth that it hurts, and find a way to prepare for better days.

Are you curious about what I did to end up in federal prison? I've resisted confessing my crimes to you during the entire process of writing this book, but I refuse to be fake, so I will be brave: I robbed banks. All by myself, in 1995. How I got to that point is a very long sordid story and not appropriate for this book, but I will say this: I wanted to die and robbing banks was my suicide mission. I decided that being killed in an armed robbery was more honorable than taking my own life, however insane that may sound. I had a major gambling problem, drug addiction, and I had this twisted 'survival of the fittest' mindset that if I was going to go out, I'd go out *big*.

I was sick in so many ways. The FBI was hunting me down and when they finally found me I was grateful. I don't take what I did lightly, I know I terrified a lot of people. I took 100% responsibility for what I did, served my time, asked for forgiveness and have spent my life serving to pay back the wrong I've done. That was over 20 years ago and I still make payments every month to pay all of the money back. Restitution matters to me, and I want to inspire any others out there who have stolen to give back to the society we took from. Yes, I was a bank robber. No, I'm not proud of it. But I decided a long time ago to trust in who I am *today* and never let my past stop me from being who God made me to be.

Our culture constantly tells us we don't need a man. I'm kind of getting tired of being beaten over the head with that opinion, as if wanting a man is some sign of weakness. I'm not saying that men define us or that we should be dependent on them in any unhealthy way. I'm also not stating that we need a man to 'complete us'. Not, at least, in the way that makes us whole as an individual. Let's just shift our perspective a little and be more compassionate towards each other about our desire, as women, to find the right guy. We need each other to figure this thing out.

We waste far too much time and energy judging each other as women. We claim to have all this feminine strength, but we rarely get real or go deep with each other, and we gossip about each other way too much. I came home from prison a new woman; ready to conquer the world, sorry for the things I had done. I was determined, focused and free…yet I couldn't find a friend to save my life. I was rejected by women in my own church because of my past *and* by feminist groups outside of church because I was a Christian. I didn't fit in anywhere. I didn't even 'look' like a criminal but when they heard about my past, there was no 'empowerment' anything, and it crushed me. I didn't stay crushed, though, because I remembered my commitment to myself, and God, and those broken women in prison: *I was going to make a difference.*

I started to pursue the truth about who I am as a woman and what kind of man I wanted to marry, and grew in wisdom. In time, I finally developed friendships with some extraordinary women who loved me unconditionally, including some successful women leaders. As much as you may not like to hear it, there is very little difference between women in prison or those with highly successful careers, when it comes to our hopes and dreams.

We are all women that want to be loved. That is a common desire that binds us, and it should. Some of us did not pay as great of a consequence for our mistakes in the pursuit of love and marriage, and some of us paid a huge price with an even greater cost to our children for generations to come. Many of us used something to numb the pain. *The only difference between us is the cost of our pain, and the variations of how we dealt with it.* I have seen the poorest of women have the richest of marriages, and I have been great friends with the richest of women in the poorest of marriages.

Let's level the playing field. As we get closer to beginning our journey, let's focus on our similarities and not our differences. Our division is the enemy, not men. Our sisterhood is the solution.

Once I discovered WHY men behave the way they do, the things that were once so hard to do in my marriage suddenly became way easier. Understanding their masculinity and our femininity and how to use them both is the key to finding and keeping a good man. Before you freak out about using their masculinity for our good, just chill for a sec: I'm going to tease this thing apart while providing real life stories to help you understand why, with action steps in a later chapter.

Why men behave the way they do created this freedom for me to be who I was craving to be: strong, bold, vivacious, while also being softer and cared for. We *can* be the badass boss babe AND still allow him to protect and provide, without comprising anyone or anything. Why do we assume we have to?

Living in Full Color

I was never able to shut my mouth because I equated being quiet with *losing* and I hated losing. I was never able to stop trying to make my point, because I *needed* to be heard. I had to keep control in a relationship because my way was the best way and frankly, the only way. Control was safer. Sex was on my time and on my terms when I had a need for control or when my self-esteem was low. I would have sex before even knowing the guy, and then after sex, wonder why I felt so used.

Before the abusive relationship, I projected the illusion that I was powerful and no one was going to tell me what to do. During the abuse, I was compromising my entire being out of a desperate need to be loved. After the abuse, I become a bitter shrew, a hunter, predator, subconsciously making all men pay for what had been done to me. Neither of these attitudes worked.

For us to discover why things aren't working we must first examine the belief system that has gotten us in this mess in the first place. We must admit responsibility for our part in this, and we can no longer blindly believe *anything*. We must come to a halt, intentionally be *awake* and ponder what this book is about.

Before opening my eyes, my life had become like a black and white version of the film 'Groundhog Day'. I was living the same day, in prison or out, over and over again, with different characters but always the same scenes: colorless, depressing, trapped in negativity without any real progress towards my desires. I tried plenty of things that worked temporarily but just like the movie I'd wake up each next morning to the same damn day without any lasting change in a different direction. I was trapped in a life of mediocre relationships at best. I realized I couldn't change the people that kept showing up in the scenes. They were all different people but somehow all the *same*. Sound familiar? *The only way to finally live the life my heart and soul craved was to change me.*

I want women to live in *full color* – not black and white. I want us to break the cycle that women are trapped in or getting sucked into. I want us to appreciate our similarities as women and celebrate the differences in men. Let's find out what a good man is, and how we can turn this mother-trucker around. Let's have pleasurable, fulfilling relationships that aren't so *hard* to manage. Girl, let's have some fun that *lasts*, a life full of excitement and adventure *with* the man we love.

Stop Overthinking

The tools I will give you to find and/or keep a good man will work because these tools are *fit* for the job. *You need the right tool for the job*, as they say. You can't use a hammer to cut down a tree, you need a damn saw. I am going to give you the saw. Don't fret over how the saw works…if it gets you the desired results, use the fricken' saw. Don't waste time over why this stuff works on a man. YOU ARE NOT A MAN so you might never really comprehend it. Just embody the source of power you *do* have, trust that these tools will work with men because men are, by design, different from women…then claim your happy result!

Listen sister, when I saw it, tried it and then *produced real results* with these tools after years of using the wrong ones, I've got to tell you, *those moments were ecstasy.* Yes, as satisfying as an orgasm. The humility it takes to honor his masculinity was NOTHING compared to the deep, fulfilling satisfaction of that gratifying result. I was getting that on-fire marriage that most women dream of! That I had dreamed of! I'm living proof it's possible.

We need to get over ourselves, eat a little dirt sometimes. It doesn't define us as dirty and it usually has some iron in it, which is good for you! As women we have elevated ourselves to the brink of insanity. We have an oversensitive, easily-triggered approach to what we will or won't do. We are so bent on being right and respected its made a lot of us handicapped, as our myopic perspective and bitter unwillingness to yield or submit to male leadership at all has become an obstacle blocking much progress. That's not power, that's weakness.

Meekness is strength under control, it is not weakness, as well. We could use a little meekness. We need to get off our high horse and let him ride us into the sunset. You'll complain if he doesn't anyway, so *let* him. And if you don't have a 'him' yet that's ok because we are going to have fun getting you ready for him. Also it can't be your way or the highway with him, you will have to work *with* the good man or *both* of you will get bucked off the white horse on your way into Happily Ever After. I still believe in

27

Happily Ever After—the mature version, not the fantasy—and it's ok to still believe in your Prince Charming.

Michael and I have ridden off into the sunset. It's romantic and dreamy and every day is an adventure. But make no mistake, I do want to punch him sometimes. He can act like an a**hole on occasion. We call each other our 'twin' because we have very similar, driven personalities. People are amazed we work so closely together and not kill each other. It's a great testament to what's possible. I love it when I hear someone say, 'I want a marriage like yours and Michael's.' I will often hear one of the women I mentor say, 'Hashtag relationship goals,' when they see Michael and I publicly walk out a tough marital moment. Considering where we both came from, our lives are a miracle. It was hell on earth for a season, but we stuck together because our common mission is to inspire others to live in excellence and abundance.

Nothing good comes easily. Growth comes from the uncomfortable. I dare you to try something wildly different during this process. I dare you to be open and listen to your feminine voice that will testify to the truths we discover about men.

Men are designed to love, protect, compete, provide and serve. *Let* them. It's *why* they exist, and it is what they were designed to do. I'm freer because I understand men now. My constant inquiry allowed me to continue to observe and think. My introspection woke me, and kept me from being led like a sheep to the slaughter. Stay curious because it will keep your mind open to new evidence and new possibilities, as well. I care about your freedom because I want you to be *happy*.

I've seen more heartbreak than most. I've seen so much evil in the world it would make you sick. I've held the hand of an adult woman as she wailed for hours over being raped by her biological father hundreds of times. I've rocked a girl to sleep in my arms that spent 7 years living in the back of a semi-truck where her uncle raped her daily. I have dried the tears of an executive woman when she found out she'd been cheated on for years. I've bandaged the wounds of a stay-at-home mom who never thought her husband would hit her. I have walked many women through the grief of losing their children because they wouldn't leave an abusive man. I'm familiar with the dark side very well… *yet I still believe there are good men in this world.* I am championing them and praying for more to stand boldly for who they are.

I do not live in the 'land of lollipops' as my ten-year-old daughter calls it, a world where people are unaware of the evil that surrounds them. My daughter thanks me for not sheltering her from this evil to the degree her classmates are sheltered because she says she is more prepared to plan for a good life. Our little girls need us to demonstrate love for ourselves in a way that honors men so they, too, can prepare for a good man.

I am thankfully and humbly very aware of the level of suffering in the people that surround us, only so that I can help them through it. Everyone's personal hurt is their own and is not ours to judge how big or small it is. I am here for you when you are waiting for him to say, "I'm sorry." I am here for you when you've climbed the ladder to success and found you are still missing something. I am here for you when you've mistakenly followed bad advice that makes you feel good for the short term but then sends you home to an unhappy relationship that is sucking the life out of you and setting a bad example for your children.

Remember: being loved is satisfying but it takes sacrifice to really have the kind of love that lasts. We have to balance taking care of ourselves with sacrificing some of our own wants so we can serve our men. It takes maturity to know where that balance is. Relationships are a two-way street we have often tried to make a one-way direction. You know what that kind of relationship is called? A childish one. Sacrifice your feelings already. Just trust me on this…you can always go back to your sucky relationship or loneliness later if my advice doesn't work. Maybe you're a married woman who wants more spice in her marriage. There is definitely more we can do so let's spice up your relationship. Getting ready for Mr. Right is exciting; keeping Mr. Right can be, too. You have *one* life. Let's live it with a sacrificial love, a great love, that has meaning and joyfully fulfills us.

When we understand who we are as women and who we were designed to be, we will break through the glass ceiling we're so desperate to shatter, we'll raise our boys to become good honorable men, we will create good futures for our daughters and we'll find and/or keep that good man for ourselves. Let's do *THAT!*

Newton's First Law

Newton's first law of motion: an object at rest stays at rest and an object in motion stays in motion with the same speed and in the same direction unless acted upon by an outside unbalanced force. Why am I talking about Newton's first law? Because this law of physics also relates to our emotions, attitudes and habits.

If we are in motion in a direction at a steady speed, we will not change unless there is an external, unbalanced force introduced. If someone has been doing things a certain way for a long time, the first law suggests it is easier to continue doing them that way than to introduce a different or alternative way of doing things.

As a culture we are in a high-speed forward motion towards denigrating masculinity and adopting radical feminism. We will stay in that motion until an external force is introduced. One intent of this book is to *be* that external force.

I'm not alone in this desire: there is a rising tide of good women saying *no* to the denigration of masculinity. The popularity of the number one top-rated TV show *Last Man Standing*, a comedy about a man trying to be a masculine man surrounded by women, proves that men are desperate for some support in this issue as well. There are extraordinary people using their voice to take a stand against what mainstream media is doing to our men, young men and boys of today. I am standing shoulder-to-shoulder with these women because we need good men for society to thrive.

Don't fall blindly for the idea that we need to change the way *men* are for *women* to excel. Don't drink the Kool Aid, girl, it's laced with the very poison that is killing off all our good men. If that philosophy was working, then where are all the good men going? If you have a problem with me saying that a good man is hard to find, take a poll: women would agree, and you know what, so would the good men.

You Can Handle the Truth

My husband swears you cannot handle the truth in this part of the book. He said I would lose you before I even get a chance to share the good advice with you. You see, I need to explain to you that you likely were not prepared to be in a relationship in the first place. Michael cautioned me because he thinks women are sensitive and won't want to look too deeply into how unprepared we really are to find a good man.

Michael is wrong. You know why? He's a man. He's designed to protect women. It's his knee-jerk reaction to make me feel good about myself. Now, I take a ton of counsel from my husband when appropriate. However, in our house and in the organization, we have a rule that men process with men and women process with women; no exceptions. Why? Because we have learned very well that we're so *different*.

Women need to stick with good women, trusting and leaning on each other, because good women will tell you what's up and speak into your life. So, here it is girlfriend: *men are our prize*. Men are one way we reward ourselves. It sounds bad, I know, but it's just reality. A good man is one major object of our success. Not the same as a trophy wife, but similar. *The man we choose to give ourselves to reflects what we believe about ourselves.* When we choose a man, we got the best keepsake we thought we could get, period. Think about it. We attract what we believe we are worth.

If we thought we were worth more, we wouldn't have attracted a man that would hurt us. It wasn't you *personally* that he didn't want, or hit, or cheated on. *He is simply a mirror of how you feel about yourself.* You chose an unprepared man because you were an unprepared woman. *Yikes.*

If your relationship is in chaos or despair, there is no way around it: neither of you were qualified. There are some minor exceptions where there truly is a qualified man that married an unqualified woman or vice versa but this is a rare, and I mean a very rare situation, so be careful before you count yourself in that category and miss the opportunity to honestly and truly examine your own readiness. It's so rare because even if a woman that seems to have it all together as a good woman marries or commits to an unqualified man there must be an area of her life she hasn't mastered, otherwise *she wouldn't have married an unprepared guy.* Make sense? Read it again if you must. Let me break it down how we would on the street, "Girl, you'd NEVER have married that loser if you had your own sh** together." Plain enough?

Haven't you ever wondered why some beautiful woman (who looks like she could get anyone she wants) shows up with some guy that doesn't have a job or even a car? It happens a lot these days, with all types of women. When you ask her why, she will have a ready list of how great he *really* is and a ready excuse that he's just in a temporary rut or it's not his fault that something unforeseen happened to him. *Ugh.* Girl, he is running game on you!

If we can just step back from our emotions and take an honest look at our current relationship (or toxic ones in the past) objectively, *we can begin to be set free and move through the hurt.* If we can see it from the lens of whether you were prepared or *not* prepared to be in the relationship in the first place, we can bring that fact into the light, learn from it and not be so devastated over the outcome.

When I realized that it was this simple of a formula—that all it was is that I was *not* emotionally and psychologically prepared to identify, attract or be with a good man—then I was able to *not* be so personally hurt by his rejection, or even his abuse. Further, realizing the man I chose to be with was *also* not emotionally and psychologically prepared to be with *me* was a huge relief. When I removed all the 'feelings' about the failed relationships and looked at our lack of preparedness as a fact, the resulting failure made sense, logically. It wasn't just *me*, it was *all* women he had been with. He wasn't prepared so he didn't know *how* to treat me, and I didn't *know* how to be treated or treat him. Get it? I hope so, sister, because this new truth can be life changing, allowing you to move past the pain and start getting *prepared*.

That's why I am here; to be a trainer. It's what I do for a living, train women to be badass women to find badass men. Pretty simple! Fun fact: once you are qualified badass woman, the badass man will find *you*.

Getting Trained

My job here is to give you the right tools and train you how to use them. To be prepared means that you have mastered the areas we are going to address in coming chapters and are skilled at identifying a prepared man.

Think of our journey as a boot camp Navy Seals kind of training. I'm not interested in training the faint at heart, those women aren't going to like this book anyway. Change requires determination. You can feel weak while going through the process, that's expected, but your tenacity and faith will carry you through to the finish.

Tough women can handle the truth and are willing to be uncomfortable and press on in the face of fear. I am calling out the courageous and mighty women that are hungry for change and willing to wrestle with me through the fire of transformation. It takes fire to refine us and if we allow it to burn off our impurities, we will come out the other side as precious gold.

You will be sore at first; your mind, body and soul will get weary during our training. Your wounds will be re-exposed, and you may feel raw at times. Oh, but in the end you will feel like a seasoned athlete, powerful, alive, ready to go after your dreams and build the life you've always wanted.

The wounded and hurt are welcome here, but I won't let you stay that way, you are better than that. So, suit up and suck it up, girl, you can handle the truth.

Chapter 3

Where Have All The Good Men Gone?

I want you to NOT think of an elephant. I do *not* want you to think of an elephant standing in the middle of the room. Stop thinking of an elephant. Do not think of an elephant with a safari hat on. I said do NOT think of an elephant in the room with a safari hat on. Are you thinking of an elephant with a safari hat on? Of course, you are. No matter how many times I have heard Michael use this in one of his classes, as hard as I try, I cannot NOT think of that damn elephant with that damn safari hat on.

I am reminded of this when I think about how we see men these days. We are constantly focusing on them as *the problem*. There is such a steady flow of male-bashing in the media, and we women habitually poke fun together at their 'defects', that it's almost impossible to *not* think of men without thinking about their 'flaws.'

Male-sympathizing is almost non-existent. As a woman, if you're caught male-sympathizing, you can expect an attack from other women, swift and harsh. The hypocrisy is so accepted, we can't even see it for what it is; we want to be honored and respected, yet we dishonor and disrespect them. As women we are so focused on elevating ourselves that any compliment of man's masculine qualities can be taken as an *offense* to women. It's a national epidemic and we hold ourselves in such high regard as we're doing it. We then model this ugly attitude to our daughters and at the same time, we are dishonoring our sons and denigrating their identities and don't even realize it. Oh boy, are we in trouble.

Where It All Started

Remember, this part of the book is about addressing the problem and then we will get to the solution. Hang on to your seats, I might really piss you off. If I have done my job, I have laid down enough sense that you trust me to continue. I am taking a risk too! I'm opposing the current views of radical feminists or those that want to diminish gender roles and they are a fierce group of people who seem to have a lot of time on their hands to make a whole lot of noise, deafening the voices of reason. Stay in touch with your inner responses and keep an open mind through this

Quick history lesson: The Industrial Revolution was the beginning of the shift that sent us in this direction. Up until then, men worked close to home, on the land, raising our sons and daughters *with* us. When the automobile was invented, men began to work more in factories in cities, and due to the working conditions they were rarely home.

Then came World War I and World War II, causing even fewer men to be an example at home of what a man is, what he does, how he treats women and how he leads his family. Men were unable to teach their sons how to become hunters and gatherers, or to teach their daughters what a good man behaves like. Mothers, bless their hearts, had to step in to raise the children alone.

Over time, the sons began to be feminized. The mothers did the best they could, but a woman cannot, back then or even today, teach a boy how to be a man. Period. There is no debate about it: women are not men and it psychologically impossible to 'think' or demonstrate manhood when you are in fact, a woman.

As a single mom, this was *so* difficult to hear. I fought the truth, ignored the evidence and rationalized it away. I got angry at anyone that said a woman needed a man to raise a boy. It seemed degrading. Somehow it was easier to accept that a man couldn't raise a girl into a woman (he can contribute and do his very best but a girl needs a woman to help her become one) than to accept that a woman couldn't raise a boy into a man. It doesn't matter how much we fight against it, it's true and our current state of affairs is the evidence. We agreed that a good man is hard to find, right? Well...this is one major reason why.

It's not our fault, moms. We weren't intended to raise our children alone, and damn it, we *are* amazing! Pat yourself on the back. Good job, mama! God knows, I know how hard it is: I worked 12-hour days, had a nice car, and a clean home before I turned to drugs and gave up, yet my eldest daughter rebelled for a long time and had no respect for what it was like to be a single mom. Additionally, I was bitter about what her father had done and the huge price I had paid for loving him. When I get home from prison, I tried to hide that bitterness from her but it leaked out and so I raised a bitter daughter. She's 23 now, and my best friend. She's married and has changed her thinking, too, and is a kind and loving mother to her two small children. Not that long ago, she looked at me and said, "Mom, I had no idea you worked so hard for us. I'm sorry for not understanding." Now that was worth its weight in gold. I thought she'd be 50 before I heard that from her. Single moms have it the hardest, which is so why we have to have a plan.

Listen. As a culture, we have raised feminized boys and we don't like to face it or admit it. If we were to be *REALLY* honest, we've even allowed our boys to replace our need for a man at times. We don't like to admit it, but we do. Often, we are completely unaware we are doing it. I don't mean in a sexual way, of course, but we do lean on our sons in some unhealthy ways at times. We nurture them to keep them happy, we coddle them to make them comfortable, and we over-parent them out of guilt because of the absence of a good father. We baby the daylights out of them. Why? We overcompensate for their hurt and often don't want them to leave so we aren't alone again. Think about it, if our sons didn't *need* a good man than why do we overcompensate for one? It's ok, say it. *My children need/ed a good father.*

For some of you, it's easy to admit. Others of you will deny the truth and fight me to the death that your child doesn't need anyone but you. For myself, the mere words passing across my lips stung so badly I became defensive at every turn. The thought that my children needed a good man only reinforced the pain I just couldn't get over. Some of you mamas reached out to a male mentor, and with their help, were able to raise your boys into good men. Some of you were just blessed that, miraculously, your son turned out well. Of course there can be exceptions to what I am saying, but let's not lie to ourselves: if your son struggles to keep a job, is overly sensitive or emotional, is insecure, if he isn't a good provider or is a complainer, abuser, cheater or an addict, then, mama, don't defend it. Don't ignore the evidence or lie to yourself about what kind of man you raised. Let's just bravely admit it and figure this thing out together.

This is likely to be the most sensitive issue out of any other I'll bring up. *These are our babies I'm talking about!* I know, I protect mine just as fiercely. But we need to come to grips with the reality that there are many generations of sons being raised these days without fathers. Please don't get me wrong, I made so many mistakes as a mother myself, along the way. I swam in guilt daily. Eventually I grew up and took responsibility for the suffering my child endured, pulling my head out of the sand so my choices didn't necessarily end up being a death sentence for my children. I ended up loving Chelsea and my future children and grandchildren in such a way that the cycle of suffering was broken and joy was released into their lives. *This* is my legacy as a mother, not the woman I buried.

But this is not a book about parenting, and I am not pointing this out to poke at your wounds or state the obvious. I want us to understand what is happening and that there is a solution. If you are a single mother, it's important for your children to have a good solid male role model in a good man, and there are ways to actively pursue that mentoring relationship for your kids without having to be 'in a relationship' with the man. Let's just acknowledge your son's need, so we can help break the cycle or avoid it altogether.

Being a good wife, however, *should be your number one focus* (even over being a good mom—whether you're married yet or not) *because more is learned by being caught than taught*, and your children are watching and will model your behaviors. My mom yelled and nagged at my dad a lot so I ended up yelling and nagging a lot, which was destructive to my relationships. Then Chelsea defaulted to yelling and nagging a lot, too, so she must be intentional about catching herself. I could never hear or receive my mother's lessons because the tone of her delivery deafened me, literally and figuratively. I couldn't see how much she loved my father because her belittling words to him drowned out any terms of endearment. My parents' story was one of love lost along the way. After 33 years of marriage, they divorced, so unnecessarily, and she died an early, sad death at the age of 53. There is a high price for our families if we don't take heed. At the *end* of my life, I don't want to be divorced from the *love* of my life.

Facing Extinction

Good men have become an endangered species; we are quick to agree on this point. In fact, you can find most women standing on their feet, hooting and hollering about this one. We collectively connect on the fact that we are losing our good men, like it's one big shared joke. We laugh contemptuously at the countless ways a man fails us and then we get our panties in a wad when we can't find the good one of our fantasies: you know, the guy you've been hoping for, that stands by your side, treasures you, makes you feel safe, AND brings home the bacon…yeah, *that* guy! And then we get bent when he doesn't fry it up in the pan, too. *He doesn't HAVE to.* But I can tell you this though, *a good woman can make him WANT to.*

Isn't that what feminism all about, our voice? Well, damn it, having a voice doesn't give us the right to have it both ways: belittling men as a regular pastime and then crying a river when we can't find a good one. Our words and attitudes are like a cancer that has spread throughout our culture, killing off the good men, because, make no mistake, our words have *impact*. Those words reflect the attitudes that affect anyone within hearing range, including the next generation of men—*our boys*.

Hey, I've joined in on the male-bashing. I've hopped in the male-bashing boat. I was bitter, and male-bashing made me *feel* better. But *THAT* boat is sinking. I understand now that I don't have to carry the weight of life alone. God made man and man is *good*. A good man can row the boat *with* you, help you navigate troubled waters and yes, even carry you to shore if you get hurt (don't make that a bad thing, you *know* you want him to carry you).

What's most puzzling is that we are so divided over *why* we are losing good men when the evidence is right in front of our faces. *If we all agree that good men are hard to find then why is it so hard to admit we must be doing something wrong, as a culture?* If male-bashing is everywhere we look (if you think I am exaggerating, you're not listening) and good men are hard to find, and we are constantly complaining about who they are NOT, then why can't we pause and look at one common denominator—*women*? It's not complicated at all.

Have we become so self-serving we can't see our own part in the problem? I wasn't always willing to look at it either. Blame was my favorite game, until the pain got too strong to ignore. When I turned my focus from my own pain to that of my sisters, I saw suffering all around me. I noticed entire families hurting and in despair because of unhappy marriages and divorce. I had to stop buying in to the blame game being prescribed to us. It can't be all their fault, *it takes two to tango.*

Girlfriend, I refuse to be a victim with you, I won't burn my bra with you, and I won't sit quietly while you bash men. Think about it: there are honorable men, *and* women for that matter, in blue out there protecting us, and veterans out there fighting for our freedom. I won't dishonor them! Yes, I won't let a bad man use you as a doormat, but I will also kick your ass if I have to, to wake you up from the crap that gets shoved down our throat every day to open your eyes to a better way to get what you want!

Our Men Are Killing Themselves

Two-thirds of all the world's suicides are by men. The rate of suicide among middle-aged men between 45-54 is dramatically on the rise. According to suicide prevention expert Dr. Christine Moutier, white, middle-aged men account for 70% of deaths from suicide each year. Nine-tenths of the male suicides are from a lower socioeconomic class.

Many psychologists blame masculinity. They blame the way boys are being socialized today and that boys' ability to express their emotions are being undermined. I call bullshit. Oh boy, do I want to say all kinds of bad words right now, this is the best-behaved I can be right now. If I am the last woman on the planet calling bullshit, fine. Think I am a little passionate on the subject? Yes, and it's a righteous anger.

LISTEN: This makes me absolutely crazy and I don't care how I come across expressing it. Our men are KILLING THEM-SELVES. If women are emotional beings, we should be getting *very* upset that our men are dying. Why aren't we? We can't fix men directly ourselves, but we can sure as hell do our part as women and as a society to find out how we are contributing. We must be brave enough to look at the evidence, take responsibility and not passively stand by and watch our sons, brothers and fathers *kill* themselves. If we keep thinking this way, nothing will change. If we accept things as they are, we are complacent, even complicit. I'll get off this tough subject in a second but if you are going to be the kind of honorable woman deserving of a good man or keep the one you got, we had *better* figure this stuff out. It affects every part of our lives.

If you are *a selfish* woman or not desiring a committed relationship, then I am likely irritating you right now. Let's be careful to not claim we want to have the love of a good man but not care what the heck is happening to our men, the good men *and* the not-so-ready kind of men. I don't care about being right. I care that we have a SILENT KILLER and not enough good women are talking about it.

Here's an interesting thought: how can suicide be on the RISE if men are more EMOTIONAL TODAY than ever before in history?

It makes no damn sense, if the 'experts' are to be believed. If there are *fewer* masculine men than EVER, then why are *more* men killing themselves, and why are we still blaming masculinity? Some experts argue that men are suffering from an eroded sense of self and identity. HELLO? That we can agree on. *We are emasculating our men, when they have been born to be masculine.* Of course it's eroding their sense of identity.

And guess what the answer mainstream psychologists are giving? They are actually suggesting that we redefine our modern definition of masculinity and become a more gender-neutral society. What the 'f ' is going on? The very reason you picked up this book proves it will never work. *Not without more of our men killing themselves.* I feel like we live on some twisted parallel world or this is all some cosmic joke in a dream we can't wake up from. How are we even allowing this message about toxic masculinity to be heard? We better wake up!

I know I sound loud and passionate right now but at least I'm *talking* about it. Women are in denial if they buy into this gender neutral crap. I am not here to judge, just to be your feminine drill sergeant to wake you the hell up. Do we *really* want our men to be gender neutral? I don't! I've spoken to hundreds of women over the years that care deeply for their men, short of a few crazies trying to shove these messages down our throat. It's cruel, it's misguided, and it's the height of arrogance on our part.

It's not our job, either. Men are not dying because they *aren't* able to express themselves. They are dying because we are changing the rules when we have no authority to do so. Hell yes, men are dying from an eroded sense of self and identity—because *society is trying to make them into something they are NOT.*

A Fatherless Generation

We need *more* masculinity in the world, *not* less. Masculinity in itself is not toxic, just as feminity in itself isn't toxic. Masculinity isn't the problem. Let's not throw the baby out with the bath water. The stripping of their manhood is the problem. When we remove who they are designed to be by denigrating it in our society, we cause confusion, depression and suicide. When a boy grows up not knowing how to be a man, confused by the messaging of the world, unprepared to compete, provide and protect, they've been set up to fail. Let men be men and they will stop killing themselves. Respect them, honor them, give them the space to grow emotionally with OTHER MEN and leave them the hell alone. As a society we have been disarming them before sending them to the battle. Life *is* the battleground.

We agree that men need the space to release their emotions, *but women want them to process the way women do*. It doesn't work since men don't process the same way as women, no matter how much we *want* them to or how much it sounds like a clever idea. I believe this idea of men processing the same as women is perpetuated by bitter women and childlike men that don't want to take full responsibility.

I do not know *one* woman that truly wants a weak and passive man. We might like it for about five minutes, then we'd be repulsed. It's appropriate for men to process their emotions in a masculine way. If men create strong bonds with other good men, there is a healthy safe space for them to be empathized with and guided. It's tribal if handled correctly but it's NONE OF OUR BUSINESS, as women. We don't get it both ways: we don't get to be attracted to a strong, confident, protector and provider and then tell him he needs to be more like a woman and express more emotions. It's not fair to them, and it's ridiculous, really. The very masculine traits that make him into the man we are truthfully attracted to are the things we are trying to strip him of.

Let's be honest: all the things we want in a man requires grit, guts, strength and fortitude. That isn't easy stuff. And men want to be that guy, innately. So, when we try to redefine masculinity or make it toxic or force gender neutrality, do you know what we produce? Weak and passive men. Do you know what weak and passive men do? They allow evil men to prevail.

We need masculinity for our society to thrive. It's what drives a man to respectfully open a door for a woman, to protect his family, to work long hours to provide and to step in front of a bullet to defend our freedom. Masculinity builds leaders, warriors, heroes and good fathers. Bad men do *not* stop being bad when we strip them of their masculinity, but they are stopped by good men that have harnessed their masculinity for *good.*

Let men be noble. Let them be what we need them to be; what we are *waiting* for them to be.

63% of youth suicides are from fatherless homes (US Dept. Of Health/Census) – 5 times the average.

90% of all homeless and runaway children are from fatherless homes – 32 times the average.

85% of all children who show behavior disorders come from fatherless homes – 20 times the average. (Center for Disease Control)

80% of rapists with anger problems come from fatherless homes

–14 times the average. (Justice & Behavior, Vol 14, p. 403-26)

71% of all high school dropouts come from fatherless homes

– 9 times the average. (National Principals Association Report)

On behalf of our future generations, it is time to take a stand.

A Rite to Pass

We lost our way when we stopped acknowledging the necessity of tradition and the importance of rituals. Many young women today have no idea of the traditional rites of passage in history, how roles were defined, and how they marked the passage of children into adulthood.

Arnold van Gennep's major work, *The Rites of Passage'*, states that rites of passage exist 'in order to consolidate social ties, establish roles, and give members of a group a sense of purpose and placement.' Ceremonies that mark important transitional periods in a person's life: birth, puberty, marriage, having children, and even death, are also key in establishing a person's identity within the world. Rites of passage usually involve ritual activities and teachings designed to strip individuals of their original roles and prepare them for new roles. Did you notice that the only rite of passage that we have abandoned today is the rite of passage into adulthood? For *both* genders? (Remember, good men are hard to find.)

By abandoning that rite of passage into adulthood, we have found ourselves living in a world filled with confused children living in adult bodies, inner children that respond in an emotionally immature way to pain and discomfort. Most social issues today can be traced back to the fact that we have not grown up, we are adult children responding accordingly. The immature, emotional response to pain is an epidemic these days.

Addiction. Abuse. Divorce. Gangs. I could list more, but you get my point: immaturity is at the heart of these issues. You know what the most compelling evidence of all is? Those that oppose the truth of my words emotionally and immaturely refuse to take responsibility for their part in all this mess. Maybe it is you. Maybe that's the 'unprepared, unready or unwilling to enter adulthood' man you chose to be with or marry or its your parents who raised you. Since misery loves company, maybe it's most of the people you know and are associated with. Maybe you have locked yourself in a kindergarten room filled with adult children friends of yours and you are all trying to play house. We can't solve adult problems with the emotional level of maturity of a child because life delivers consequences. Sometimes the consequences are subtle, but sometimes, like mine were, they are loud and hard.

I'm most sad for those that have the subtler consequences because a person slowly bleeding has the hardest time finding the source of the bleed. It's the deadliest because we don't even know we are dying until it's almost too late. When you feel like you were just sawed in half from the pain of the consequences of refusing to grow up, the source of the problem is obvious and in your face, so it's easier to change.

A lot of us are just plain brats: little girls and boys wanting our own way. Without the clean break from our childhood and the clear passing into adulthood, we never learn to appreciate the power of pain and its purpose in guiding us, or how to have courage in the face of fear. Our marriages fail because we don't know how to commit to stick through the hard times. Our future generations are never taught to grow up either. We become children having children.

If how we operated as a culture before was so *bad*, then why were there so many more good men available back then? Because they were men of honor, despite the social issues we were struggling with at the time. I am not saying we didn't have problems as a society. Every generation has their own need for growth. Discrimination isn't something any of us were proud of. Clearly, we have made progress as a society and we still can continue to grow, but I am suggesting that we can't if we don't grow up.

In the early years of childhood, a boy bonding to his mother is vital to his growth. By age 6, however, he looks for the nearest male and starts to study what to do. By age 14, there is an 800% increase in testosterone, which is a challenge for a boy becoming a man, especially without a male guide. Men need men. It is their right to pass into adulthood and they need a rite of passage to help define for them what a good man is, what we are waiting for them to be, and what we *need* them to be.

Letting Our Sons Go

One of the greatest challenges in my life, despite my crazy past, was to stay out of the process of my husband becoming a better man by allowing him to stumble...or even fall...as he was learning to be a good father. (He would have never let me rescue him anyways.) I had to stand by and watch my husband make mistake after mistake when he lost his temper with our son (no he didn't beat him). I had to keep my mouth shut as Michael faced the painful fact that, in many ways, he was behaving like the father he had once despised...then witness the sting as that realization hit my husband in the gut, after seeing the look of wounded hurt in our son's eyes.

My heart ached over and over through the process. It's in my nature to nurture them both. In the beginning, I would instinctively run to my husband and son when something happened between them, to reach out to them both, but my husband would turn and hold his hand up. Like a wounded soldier, he would look me in the eyes and silently asked me not to interfere. I could see them both hurting, and it ripped my heart right out of my chest, but no matter how powerful of a woman I was, no matter how capable a mom or how loving I thought myself to be, I wasn't able to help my son and my husband get where they needed to go, as men.

Michael wasn't abusing me by holding me back. He wasn't trying to belittle me, diminish my abilities or disrespect me. He also wasn't trying to stop me from being my son's mother. The cold hard truth was it was none of my business. It was between them, *as men*. This was *men's* business. My son was twelve and it was time for him to leave the comforts of a nurturing mother and it was time for me to *let him go*. Loving him was letting him go.

Since the beginning of time, different cultures have taken their children through some kind of ceremony, a rite of passage into adulthood, for the purpose of establishing them in their role in the community. The rituals have varied for each culture but one thing each of them had in common was a perception of a dangerous or *an actual* dangerous circumstance for the child to face their fears and overcome them, thereby learning to put away childish things and enter into adulthood.

We've lost that traditional and important rite of passage in American society. Rituals that allowed us to face our fears, overcome them, and with that gain the appreciation of the privileges and responsibilities that come with being an adult. Without these rituals, we are left with adult children struggling without vision and understanding of their unique calling as men or women, nor their honorable responsibility to serve their community.

Thankfully, Michael brought our son through his rite of passage. He is still teaching him how to harness his masculinity for good. He prepares him to stand up to the evil men in this world and protect me closely when his father isn't around. There will always be bad men because we live in a fallen world, but our Knights in Shining Armor are masculine and are here to defend us, and they are *designed* to. It's what us women want, because it's who we *are*.

Always Be As Hot As The Mistress *Would* Be

Chapter 4

What a Man Wants

A Battle to Fight - A Beauty to Rescue - An Adventure to Live

I loved this when Michael shared it with me. What a precious picture it paints of the longings of a man. And how perfect is it that who a good man is *born* to be, is who we *want* him to be?

When I sit still and quiet my mind from the noise of the world and focus on the picture of a good man battling fiercely, rescuing his beauty and living his adventure, it makes me smile and it feels right in my soul. When I connect that picture to the man of my dreams, that image I created as a young girl, it seems so pure and innocent and good. The cognitive dissonance between my mind and my soul evaporates, cleared of the confusion of what I've

been told versus what I imagined him to be. I am at peace because *his* instinct is to be that man, and mine is to *want* that man.

Where did we get lost? Where do we go from here? How do we
mend what our culture is trying to tear apart? There's no point in
placing blame because we are all responsible for our own contri-
butions, men and women, however big or small. We've forgotten the simplicity and beauty in just being who we were designed
by the Creator to be. We've missed the mark, we've ignored our
moral compass and lost our way at times. The loss of our identities as men and women in our culture is a big issue at this point.

The better question is: Who will lead the way out? I'm raising my
hand. Sister, will you raise yours? I am raising my hand for the
sake of marriages and goodness, and on behalf of the good men
still standing, and the good men still growing up. Changing our
culture's perceptions must start with you and me. It begins with
us remembering how women and men were created to be, feminine and masculine. It begins with us women doing an about-
face and walking in honor and respect and admiration for men
in their masculinity.

Let's rediscover ourselves in the coming chapters, reevaluating
our habits of thinking and actively shifting our perspective for
the husbands we have or the true loves we long to find. Let's be
students of what makes a man a good man and stop the insanity
of trying to make him something he's not. After being with bad
and passive men, I finally married a manly kind of man, Michael.
Yet with all the understanding I have gained, and as successful
as my marriage is, I'm still tempted to want him to be something
he's not at times. And boy, oh boy, does he wish I would be something I'm not sometimes too, especially when I have snot flying
because I'm sobbing over some fear I have about our children or

the businesses we run. I used to get so upset that he didn't seem as emotional as I when there were more bills than money coming in, or our eldest was acting out, or our youngest was dealing with some mean kid at school. I'm not a needy woman, but I still get emotional, and I would get pissed at Michael for not responding the *way I was* emotionally responding. I laugh now, picturing myself in hysterics, infuriated at his calmness.

There have been many times he has calmly asked, "Would you feel safer if I was acting like you are right now?"

I'd stop, wipe my dripping nose on my sleeve and answer him with a confused look, "Well, no."

That would stop me in my tracks. *Actually, I wouldn't feel safer*, I realized. Of course I would agree inwardly, but not give him the satisfaction of knowing that I did, nor admit my appreciation for his stability. I did not want to yield to his logic, I just wanted him to act like me. Why? Why couldn't I acknowledge his effort to keep me safe?

Listen. I'm going to yell it from the mountaintops: we *can't have it both ways!* It's not right to want our man to be the same type of person that we are; it's selfish, misguided and just plain *wrong* for us to demand that of men. This relentless, persistent push against masculinity has eroded the true nature of who a man is.

We are teaching our girls (and boys) that men are 'bad and un-emotional'. From the earliest ages, we subconsciously (and then overtly) communicate to our girls that men are scary and aggressive, and we should watch out for them, and then as adults we tell our daughters to go marry one! What is this confusing message we are sending them? The media reinforces it and there's no argument from us. We really aren't addressing the issue of our perception of males or training our future generations what to look for. We send our daughters off to find a man to marry in a world where good men are facing extinction, and we send our sons out into a world of competition when no one has equipped them.

Increasingly our men are ill equipped and confused over their roles, their place in society, their identities. Women are demanding them to be their prince charming while at the same time be more emotional. We have also been known to accuse their masculinity of being just a mask that hides a man's emotions, instead of understanding their masculine differences, celebrating them and acknowledging how they serve us as women and as a community.

He Wants to Keep it Simple

Good men want simple things: love, family, sex and to be a part of something bigger than themselves. Men are not complicated beings. They are amazing and intelligent and capable but they are not *hard* to figure out, as we women are. *A good man is quite easy to satisfy and only desires to be fully accepted and trusted by the woman he loves.*

To love someone means the person giving the love receives the greatest blessing. I think we have forgotten what love really means. We ourselves want that selfless version of love, but do we *really* offer it to the man we love? Our version is more like this: *I will love and honor my man if he changes into who I have him planned to be.* Sorry girlfriend, it doesn't work that way.

You can't make him be anything. Come on, we've known this, and we have tons of proof that it's true, but we just-keep-trying to change him, because we *want* him. We like how he makes us *feel* when he is behaving the way we want him to so we want to keep him for good. We need to snap out of it: splash some water on our faces, slap ourselves, pinch ourselves, whatever it takes to shake us out of this idea that we can change him. I know it hurts because we tend to translate his unwillingness to change himself as rejection or uncaring, but it's not about US. He won't change because we are trying to change him in the way that doesn't work, never has worked, and never will…at least not in the long term.

Let's just finally admit this whole control thing OBVIOUSLY does not work. If he did change at all through our nagging and control, he won't respect us in the end or trust us or honor us or likely even stay committed to us. I will show you how to get what you want from a good man the *right* way; not by manipulation, but a way that *works* with men.

He Wants To Be Compatible

I think I could write an entire book on the issue of compatibility, alone. I personally believe this is the main culprit for the high rate of divorce. A lack of compatibility combined with an increasing shortage of good men means to me that we are only going to see the divorce rate increase if we don't get a handle on this. Compatibility is the difference between a relationship thriving or dying. The problem is in today's world we stay in dying or dead relationships *hoping* something changes.

The definition of compatibility is a harmonious relationship: well-suited. well-matched, like-minded, in tune, reconcilable.

We don't seem to consider *compatibility* when choosing a partner for a committed relationship. It's very easy when you first meet someone you find attractive to just put on your best face, be considerate and willfully ignore anything that annoys you. We hold back the darker parts of ourselves and put on our game face.

If you choose to date (or court, which we will discuss later) it will give you both some time to discover each other's compatibility, allowing the opportunity for you both to see past each other's 'good side' to find out if you are a good match. To stand the test of time, we need to have common interests and values and to align ourselves emotionally, intellectually, politically, and philosophically. We need to find out his views on sex, money, kids, parenting, in-laws, and handling conflict. We need to inquire into his willingness to support our dreams and how he will add value to our vision. Will he make us feel safe? Does he have the means to provide for a family? These are just the major questions. The little ones can make a great impact as well. What is his diet like, his communication style, his pace for life, does he like you to talk dirty to him?

Compatibility is what he's also looking for in the one he wants to *keep* and *marry*, or else we are quickly put on the short list. We'll talk about sex here soon, but sister, if you skip the courting phase you will not find out if you are *truly* compatible. Courting is a bit of a lost art form. We want a man and we want him *now*. Our desire for instant gratification is costing us so much, including a lot of time, in the long run. The relationship won't work if you both aren't compatible.

Ever heard of irreconcilable differences? They are a no-fault ground for divorce (which means neither party committed any sort of extenuating act, such as adultery, abandonment or extreme cruelty) so neither party is at fault for the breakdown of the marriage. I propose that a lack of compatibility is the irreconcilable difference. Since it is your responsibility to take this seriously, for your peace and future life and your future children, save yourself major heartache on the front end and *find out if you two are actually compatible. Try courting!*

He Wants to Trust You

Trust is the foundation for a relationship. Most of us agree on this but I believe women don't fully understand how men interpret trust. This is critical so pay very close attention: *men do not value trust the same WAY that women do.*

We compare how men trust to a woman's value system and miss the very thing that a good man is looking for in a woman. Trust to a woman involves her body. Trust to a man *involves his respect and honor.*

As women, when we hear the word 'trust', we think of fidelity, a man being faithful. We imagine trusting a man to never give himself sexually to another woman or to never touch our bodies in a violent way. When he cheats on or is violent with us, he violates our body and therefore our trust, and it breaks our heart. A woman will stand by her man for almost *anything*, even if he commits a crime...and often, even if he hurts our children in some way...that's an ugly fact. Women rationalize away the truth so we can *keep* him then proceed to live in shame about it. Girl, you know it's true and it doesn't matter where we come from, we women compromise ourselves. So our men can do just about anything and we will stay loyal, even going through hell with them, but geez, if they cheat on us? *We go crazy.* Trust to us means don't cheat or hit. We will pretty much put up with anything else.

For a man, trust is attached to his heart and his mind. *He trusts you if you accept him fully as he is.* He trusts you if you don't use his weaknesses against him in a fight. He trusts you if you respect him both publicly and privately, honoring him among others and not gossiping behind his back. He trusts you if you are faithful in the little things. A good man who trusts his woman will do *anything* for her; he will protect her and cherish her and keep her all the days of his life. Men do not want to be alone, but they want a good woman they can *trust*. Become a trustworthy woman.

For years, I was in relationships where I was cheated on. I'd check their pagers and cell phones regularly. I have followed a man to work and pathetically listened on the other side of doors trying to catch him talking to other women. I blush at the memories of how insecure and desperate I was. Maybe you weren't as bad as that, maybe it was more of a silent insecurity you expressed somehow to him. Whatever it was, none of that behavior had any real influence over whether he would actually cheat or not.

By the time I met Michael, all that behavior had been ground off me the hard way. I was at peace about the matter: if he was a cheater, nothing I said or did would change it. In fact, the more I'd try to find out if he was, the more miserable I would become, so I resolved to not focus on it at all.

I had an internal conversation with Michael about it, that went something like this:

If you are the guy I think you are, you won't cheat. If you do cheat, I can't stop you, so I am choosing to believe the best in you because you seem to have good character. If I am wrong, being paranoid and suspicious won't affect anything. The truth always comes out. So, in the meantime, I am not going to question you in any way and I'm going to relax and enjoy our time together.

Now, that internal conversation about trust was not easy for me. By the time I got to that point, I had endured tremendous suffering. Betrayal is the most severe form of rejection. Rejection is so painful that people will even take their own lives over it. It's serious stuff.

Michael used to be a contractor and often worked out of town and he didn't always have great cell service. After about 4 months together, he looks at me next to him in the truck one day and asks, "You never check up on me. Not once, ever. Do you ever question if I am where I say I am?"

I remember that question so well because it felt like I had just won a gold medal in the Trust Olympics. I had just accomplished what I had trained myself for years to do. I trusted a man, without condition, accepting him fully at his word, setting boundaries...he knew what I wanted and was clear about the life I expected him to provide, and I had honored him among men... and he, in turn, had chosen to trust me with his heart in return. It was like he hung the gold medal on me himself.

About a year ago, I asked Michael what really it did for him, what had made him certain that I was the one. He paused, silent for some time and then finally said, "You trusted me. With all that you could have questioned me about, you chose to trust, again and again. It made me want you and it made me believe I was deserving of being trusted, despite all the wrong I had done in my life. I was worthy of you because you were trusting of me."

Trust. It's different for men and women but equally as vital and valuable for us both. Our lack of trust can never make a man more trustworthy. The truth will be revealed because the darkness can't hide from the light. Live in the light. Even if he breaks your trust, which even a good man might, because life happens. And then? Then we must choose forgiveness, which we will get to in another chapter.

Trust is the foundation that he wants to build his life with you on. Trust must be written on your heart in a way that you treasure, cherish and understand how delicate it is to a man.

He Wants Your Wisdom

It's interesting to me how my husband has utilized my wisdom differently over the years. It's still a bit of a mystery to me in some ways but it's fascinating and, I think, important to mention.

The definition of wisdom is the quality of having experience, knowledge, and good judgment; the quality of being wise.

A man can be wise in his own right, but his wisdom is limited to his perspective as a man, on any matter (same for us as women). He can be the wisest of men, but he will never have a woman's experience, a woman's knowledge or a woman's intuition or good judgment. Remember, women are complicated emotionally and physically, whereas men are simpler. It would make sense that they would appreciate the wisdom of a complex creature such as ourselves. In no way am I elevating women above men because we equally have a place in the order of things here on earth. I am suggesting that we *need* each other.

Over the years, I have observed Michael act in surprising ways on the wisdom I've shared with him on a wide variety of matters. Michael is wise beyond his years and most are taken aback by his high level of intelligence. He is analytical and perceives most things unemotionally, like math equations; easy to solve. He asks God for wisdom and God most definitely gives it to him.

It's fascinating to me that often when I think he didn't hear my advice on a matter, I would find out later that he followed my suggestions.

That's wisdom on Michael's part. He is wise enough to appreciate the input I offer. He recognizes the complexity of my mind, is familiar with the valuable intuition of a woman, and appreciates the wisdom God gives me as well. That makes him a genius in my book, and I think most women would happily agree.

When he takes my advice, though, I make it a point *not* to point it out. I won't blast him with, 'Hey, that was *my* idea!' I have foolishly done that on occasion during our early years together, which was just my pride and insecurity talking. As we mature in humility and security, we don't *need* the credit. We aren't in competition with each other, we're partners who appreciate and value each other's wisdom. He does the same for me. I listen to Michael now because I understand how pride can blind a person. I see clearly now that when Michael is deciding something on my behalf or guiding me in any type of direction, that my safety (physical, emotional and psychological) is at the forefront of his mind. He often can see a few steps ahead, and I value that in him. As an abstract thinker, my head is often off in the clouds creating something, so I've learned to listen to him because, damn it, he's often right. He's stopped me from tripping and falling, in every kind of way, and on so many occasions, that I have learned to depend on his wisdom to protect me.

A good man will value your wisdom if he is wise. Let him be wise without having to applaud your own influence in his decision. Just care about the outcome we were hoping to get and not its source. Listening to each other's wisdom will take time and you both will fail at listening if you insist on always taking credit.

If you keep at it, stating your opinion, concern or solution in way that isn't demanding or aggressive, and give it time to resonate, a good man will listen and act, eventually.

Michael loves to take risks, he's adventurous. In some areas, I am less of a risk taker, especially in financial matters. Over the years I have been behind the scenes getting our house financially in order, increasing our insurance coverage, planning for a storms that could come, or whatever it took to minimize any risks so that Michael could be the risk taker he was born to be. He has done the same for me, so I could take risks in different areas. In time, I saw changes, evidence that he was heeding my advice: he learned how to take risks without overly exposing us to potential losses, he took my cues and would slowly, quietly increase the company insurance policies to save money, and he would be proactive in situations he was once reactive to. It was a learned behavior I noticed, but I never tried to rub his nose in that. I wasn't perfect at it, but I learned that trying to stop him from being adventurous or taking risks would kill him, so I chose to have his back without gloating over it.

One day, he told someone right in front of me, "If it weren't for my wife's intuition, I wouldn't be where I am today." I did a double take. After all these years, I didn't even know he knew what I was up to.

A Man Wants the Power of Agreement

This is another one between a man and woman we don't commonly discuss. It is important to acknowledge, though, because a good man will understand its power and use it wisely. Division between a man and woman can obviously lead to divorce, that's a given, but I think we ignore the power of agreement in a relationship. We tend to focus on the negative and miss out on what's possible when a married couple *agrees*. A man wants to agree with a woman because when he's willing, not by force but by that unseen strength that agreement manifests in the love between them, incredible things can happen.

Michael and I weren't together very long before we discovered the incredible energy and strength that came from being in agreement on a matter. Our children would sense this strength with our parental decisions and our families responded to it by never trying to divide us on an issue. When in agreement it was like our decisions caused the ground to shake beneath our feet. When we founded Crossing the Jordan, that powerful unity caused a kind of authority around our lives that moved mountains…and still does to this day. Not only were we compatible, our relationship was destined to be. Everyone around us could sense it. The first day we took a risk by faith and trembling, choosing to trust God with our mission, Michael looked at me and said, "I can feel it. Nothing is impossible when we are in agreement."

A man wants a woman to walk in that strength of agreement with him. We are here for a purpose, and the power between a man and a woman in agreement—on a united mission, *as one*—has a mighty impact on the world for good. Imagine what you can do together as a team, a completely united power couple, with a plan of action? This is the kind of relationship we are all longing for.

Always Be As Hot As The Mistress *Would* Be

The only thing necessary
for the triumph of evil is for
good men to do nothing..
- Edmund Burke

Chapter 5

A Good Man

Have you ever wondered if you even know who a good man is anymore? We probably have lots of preferences, tastes, and characteristics we might look for or mental snapshots of scenes swirling around in our pretty little heads. We know what bad men look like, but do we know what a good man looks like? What to intentionally seek for in him, what actions to watch for, what qualities to look for in him, or how to create a road map that can lead us to him, or better…him to us?

If you are already married, do you have vision for who you really want him to be? Not that we can change him, but as we change our thinking and actions, it influences our husbands to want to be the good man we married him to be, so we should have an idea and a hope of what we desire, to envision for our marriage.

We should have a very clear idea about what a good man is and what we want. We women have always known what we are dreaming of, so we either lie to ourselves or simply settle if we accept anything less. Women that are trying to redefine men and their masculinity have work to do on themselves way before they can try to make a change to a species that God designed.

If we open our ears and listen carefully to the pulse of our Western culture, I believe our hearts are beginning to beat again for good men, with all their true dependable masculinity and strengths that we are naturally drawn to. There is also a hunger for some of our lost traditions, rituals, our foundation as a culture. Radical feminism may have the loudest voice in the media but good women from all types of backgrounds understand there is a difference between men and women and those differences should be appreciated and celebrated. Good women understand that innately.

Let's get to know who a good man is; you've met him before, in your dreams. Let's re-introduce ourselves and make a stand for who he is and all that we want him to be.

A Good Man's Quietness

Did you know a man speaks 25% as much as a woman? Think about that. We talk 75% more in our lifetimes than a man. Holy smokes. Why? Because men process inwardly, and we process externally.

We complain that men don't communicate with us enough but it's crazy to judge them for the way in which they process. It's not bad, no more than the way women process is bad. His silence doesn't equal his disinterest, but we translate it that way most of the time. Men communicate or 'talk' in their own masculine way, differently than we do. Not always, but often it is one sign we should pay attention to when we are trying to qualify a man. Let me explain what I mean by this kind of talking.

In my many years of standing beside my husband as he guided many men into manhood, I noticed that when we first meet an immature man, they 'talk' a whole lot; they are either bragging about something or whining as a victim of their circumstances. They don't seem to know how to communicate any way other than bragging or complaining. One of the greatest joys in my life is watching the process of maturity unfold before our eyes when that lost boy finally becomes a good man. I've observed that the most profound sign that a boy is becoming a man is their 'talk' changes: they become the quiet man in the room.

A good man doesn't need to prove his worth, he doesn't need to posture himself constantly, speak aggressively or brag to reinforce his self-esteem. He knows who he is among men. He also doesn't need to process the way a woman does because he has left his mama's breast and is growing out of childish attitudes. He starts processing inwardly, secure in who he is. He is thinking. He is listening. He is trying to navigate in the right direction. He is being introspective, and wisdom comes from contemplation.

People aren't contemplators anymore. We're too busy or overstimulated, so we have to intentionally slow down. We women naturally process outwardly, so everyone knows what we are thinking! We frown upon men's silences because it's mysterious to us. We are in the dark while a man is processing inwardly, and we want to know what he is thinking! But why not let him think, let him ponder? Let's not jump to conclusions while he is silent. If he is a good man, he is surveying the land and plotting his course. If he's always talking about what he is going to do, then he isn't taking the time to think and plan how to do it. Sometimes communicating every move you make is a sign of insecurity, a way of seeking outside approval. A good man doesn't need to seek others' constant approval and will only seek out help when it's absolutely necessary. He's more concerned about getting the job done right than talking to you about it. So, let him contemplate. He can't do that while you are pushing him to verbalize more or making assumptions about what he might be thinking about.

Michael generally doesn't speak unless it's necessary. He's a 'man of few words'. Most times you'll find him in the back of the room (unless he is the speaker) with his arms crossed, eyes moving across the room. It's not obvious, but you can sense him keeping an eye on things and watching out for trouble (and not in a paranoid way). If you ask those that know him, they'll say that when Michael is in the room, people feel protected and safer knowing he's always aware of his surroundings. It's in a man's nature to protect, so Michael's just doing his thing, quietly observing, keeping an eye out.

When we go to a restaurant, Michael tends to guide me to the seat opposite the one facing the room. I used to resist, thinking he was being selfish, trying to get the better seat, until I realized why he was doing it. He's looking out for my safety. We don't mention it and no one even notices, it's just the way he moves through life, quietly protecting. Most often his silence reflects inward planning, even in those small matters like where to sit. In the early years, I'd want to shake him for not talking, and I would quiz him, asking a quick sharp question to see if he was paying attention...and 100% of the time he was present, extraordinarily so, and his responses actually proved he was more aware of the depth of our conversation, or space, or situation, than I was. It was fascinating to me, as a woman, to find that his silence had such a profound purpose...and instead of feeling ignored or rejected, I found myself feeling treasured and adored.

I don't press him to talk anymore. I'll ask to discuss a subject with him, then wait till he's ready to talk about it. He will talk when he is ready. I used to get offended, withdraw and assume that he's just not interested, but now I just talk enough for the both of us. He listens, and he is very interested because he cares about what I have to say. In fact, neither of us competes for the attention of the other, talking over each other, selfishly clamoring to be heard (I do love to be heard) because we are having quality interaction. Michael's contribution, when he really does speak, is more valuable to me because I know he has listened and processed it inwardly, and now I get the pleasure of the quality of full engagement instead of the quantity of empty words.

This doesn't just go for our men, this is true for our boys, as well. When we force our boys to share, we are basically training young men against their natural way to process, teaching them that our way is the only way to process. Let's just be careful to not make that just another way we dishonor them as males, dismissing their natural design to express themselves in a different way than we do.

By the way, a man's silent, inward way of processing isn't putting him at higher risk of mental health issues, either: that's one of our increasingly feminized cultural assumptions and pressures to make men do more of what they clearly don't naturally want to do (talk). That's what's wrong. We falsely blame the fact that men talk 75% less than women as the source of the problem, as if being more like women is the answer, and somehow more right...what arrogance!

A good man tends to process his 'stuff' with other good men. I will acknowledge there's a lack of good men for them to process with. But we contribute to this problem when we try to feminize men, and it will have a devastating effect on the survival of our society as we know it. It will get increasingly harder to find good men to support other men with their struggles or guide young men into manhood. We can do our part to help good men raise our boys but meddling with how or with whom a man works through his emotions doesn't work and it is none of our business.

Our only concern should be how women react to men's quietness and how we are making it a bad thing culturally. Men's silence and inward contemplation is necessary for a healthy community to thrive with healthy men. His quietness is not about you, it's about him.

A Good Man Leads and Protects

When I pictured a man in my life, in my mind he was holding my hand, leading us toward the mutual vision for our life, a step ahead of me to protect me from any dangers on our adventure together. Both of us are smiling, he is wanted and needed and I am desired and respected. That's the picture I wanted for my marriage, and the kind of man I wanted.

In that picture we are moving towards a mutual goal, and he was slightly ahead of me by a step because he was taking 'point'— protecting us as we moved forward. I did not picture myself leading him by the hand, controlling or dragging him towards my dream. He wasn't aggressive for leading me a step ahead and I wasn't 'weak' for following. *A man naturally wants to lead the relationship, and the family, while a woman naturally manages both.*

Why has the idea of a strong man leading his lady become so contemptuous or politically incorrect when a man leading his family is what most women want him to do? Why was that beautiful dream of wanting him to lead with strength somehow now tainted or embarrassing? Why did the mere thought of yielding to a man's leadership in any way seem like ultimate surrender, making me less of a strong person? When did my vision of what I was hoping for in a man became wrong? These are the questions I ask as I find myself swimming through a dark sea of angry women demanding their rights and refusing to yield in any way for fear of losing respect or becoming a 'doormat.' The progress of more women becoming bosses is super awesome and I'm totally loving the #girlboss vibe, but the Instagram accounts I once loved to follow are increasingly laced with bitter, acerbic undertones, and those I once thought to be inspiring are beginning to sound more like brainwashed 'victims', making our fight for equality embarrassing and weak. *We can't be both victim and victorious.*

Women are fully capable of leading a nation IF we are called and equipped to. The same goes for men. It shouldn't be a question of our ability as much as what is our God-given purpose. We have proven our worth as women over and over in education, medicine, and the sciences, among other fields. The secret to more of our successes, I believe, is to take a stand for our true femininity, recognizing its worth, while honoring masculinity's contribution as well, so ALL of our gifts and potential can be fully realized together, as a people. Then women will continue to make progress in the workplace and climb the ladder in business, or anywhere, if they so choose.

Wanting a man to lead us in our relationship doesn't make us unequal in worth. Why can we comprehend servant leadership in our careers but not let our men be servant leaders in our homes? We must stop lying to ourselves that we are attracted to a man that follows us. If he's behind us, we are stripping him of his job to protect us, and we have less respect for him as a man and less trust in his ability to protect us, making us feel insecure and unsafe…which makes us need to control things even more. On the other hand, we also can't be upset with a man for not leading us but then call him out as a tyrant when he tries to.

A true, mature person leads without a single word of acknowledgement because they do a good job, they serve others, and they rise by lifting others up. This goes for men and women. We can have both: we can have equality in the world and still be led by the man we love. Let's let the men we love be our leaders and watch our dream marriages unfold.

Michael and I are a team, we work together well. In my areas of expertise, I will lead in that situation, but I don't have to declare it or demand his acknowledgement; I just lead in that moment because we are a team. I do what needs to be done to benefit our family and move us forward, and in a manner that is honorable to him and not elevating of myself. When it's a matter of his expertise, Michael steps in and leads in the same way. We don't always do it perfectly and sometimes there's a moment of friction about the direction, but generally speaking, he leads, and I love that he does.

I am no less than my husband by my yielding to his leadership than he is less of a man by serving his family and yielding to God's leadership. A good woman knows who she is and understands that if she trusts her man's leadership, they will get to where she wants to go. That good man will serve you, take the risks with you, and lead you both towards making your dreams come true.

Together, Michael and I get to mentor and coach many people in our program. When one of them gets apprehensive about where we are leading them and how, Michael will often use this analogy, 'If you were walking on a path, and there was a snake in the road, would you want me to tell you?'

That's a picture easy to relate to. A good man leads a good woman for the purpose of seeing the snake ahead of her and then killing the S.O.B. so her pathway is clear, not because she isn't a snake slayer herself and can't do it without him but because he wants to slay the snakes—he's made to, he's good at it, and he wants to make a safe passage for her to reach her destination.

A literal example of this happened recently in San Francisco. We were walking down Market Street on a busy day, and Michael was a half-step in front of me, his standard formation when in crowded places, and our son and daughter were beside me. Out of nowhere, I see in the corner of my eye a homeless man's fist coming towards my face. At that same moment, Michael grabs my shoulder and flings me backwards, while my 6' 1" son also moves quickly beside me to make sure I didn't fall.

It all happened in a split second. My mind was still spinning to grasp what was going on when Michael started circling the homeless man, lion-like, on high alert. My son pulled his sister and I to safety, instinctively knowing his role as a young man and his father's son.

As we observed the scene now from a safe distance, my heart began to ache for the homeless man, loudly talking to himself in his dirty rags, his arms wildly gesticulating around his head, and I thought to myself, *he picked the wrong man to mess with,* as I watched my husband assessing the man calmly and unobtrusively, no one else noticing what was happening.

In the past I would have gotten involved if some sort of drama was unfolding but I have since learned to stay out of it as it's his job to protect, and not my expertise. So I didn't interfere, and after a moment Michael stopped pacing, turned back towards us and said ever-so-sweetly, "Pray for him. He needs our prayers."

My son prayed quietly as we walked to the Metreon for dinner and a movie. (We don't pray out loud to be weird or overheard.) We didn't discuss what happened, as Michael never uses these types of situations to brag about himself. They are only moments of leadership by example: leading his son how to be a man, and showing our daughter how a man protects.

A man's key role is to protect life. Why would we strip him of that?

A good man leads and protects in all areas of his life, in a similar manner. His inward contemplation allows him to plan how he is going to lead, what the best route would be and then clear the path to the destination of anything harmful that may try to hinder us from getting there…physically, mentally, emotionally or spiritually.

A good man will fight if he needs to. Among men, some kind of fighting, whether in competition or literally, shows his superiority over other men. In martial arts they teach you to fight, (and if you earn a black belt, you're taught how to kill) but above all you are taught discipline to carry yourself confidently in such a way that you don't *have* to fight. A good man operates the same way. His best guarantee of peace is his confident ability to fight: it demonstrates his competence in conflict, while simultaneously decreasing the probability that he will have to fight. This drive to preserve and protect will resonate through all areas of a good man's life.

Michael has also always been a few steps ahead of me with parenting our children, making sure that path was clear as well. Whenever there has been a tragedy, he has had the silver lining ready to point out, to comfort us in during any time of sadness. As I write this now, I'm still at an airport after 9 hours of delays and cancelled flights. I'm traveling alone, and I just called Michael to complain about how poorly United Airlines was treating me. He quickly responded with, "You're delayed? Awesome! Now you have time to write your book! It's an answer to prayer. Don't worry, I've got everything handled at home." (I laughed out loud as I was right in the middle of proofreading this chapter.)

As I walked through the terminal, I had a big smile on my face as I replied, "I'm not even going to complain anymore," I laughed, "it's useless with you. Thanks, babe, I am excited to get to write." There was that silver lining. The sky wasn't falling like the dramatic girl inside me likes to think, and anyway, I had really only called him on the phone to rescue me, because I know I'm his and he likes to rescue his beauty. I let him, and he likes that I let him.

Before you go and think I'm saying my husband is a perfect male specimen of marriage or that I'm elevating him unrealistically, let me remind you that, of course, he is still capable of being an a--hole sometimes. I'm not some dreamy, starry-eyed young girl; I've been through some serious stuff. I'm pushing near 50, I've matured the hard way and I don't live in a fantasy world. We need real life examples of good men, so we know what to look for, and Michael is one.

Heads up—*good men that are protective leaders tend to not be very agreeable*—it's what makes them assertive. Don't look at their disagreeableness as a weakness however; instead understand its purpose in a good man's drive to protect. Appreciate it, and move forward. Good men that are disagreeable won't avoid the underdeveloped areas of their lives. We can't change a man, but a good, disagreeable man will change because he will face and challenge that weakness in himself, that an agreeable man wouldn't. He will learn from his weaknesses, develop his strengths, and gain wisdom because he won't avoid the hard work of personal growth. He understands he needs to be a developed man to protect wisely.

Michael is not easily persuaded, he's slow to agree with me and then very quick with his decisions. I'd often feel threatened when he was like this, so it has taken an extraordinary amount of patient work on my self-confidence to be secure in who I am as a woman. Understanding the purpose behind this behavior, though, made me appreciate his drive and ultimately drove me to excellence as a woman. It's made me a better boss, friend, wife and mother. Michael's the CEO and President of a large, rapidly growing social enterprise and I'm his Vice President. Just imagine with me how hard it can be at times when our decision-making intersects, especially with a smart-assed mouth like mine! I've had to learn to trust his leadership and his 'NO's. Understanding that it's his job to protect us from danger allows me to rest in the comfort of his wisdom, and it has served my vision and our family well. We are a team and we run the race together.

Here's a marital secret sauce: we are never 'down' at the same time because we run like a relay team. He will pass the baton sometimes and then I will run the race for us. When Michael is weary and tired, he can set his pride aside and let me lead as he rests and refuels. He doesn't usually rest too long or take advantage of his break, he just takes in what he needs to refresh and fill up, and then picks the baton back up and continues to lead his family. He knows that I like to feel capable, and I enjoy leading at times, and stepping in occasionally is my way of giving back to him. He carries a lot on his broad shoulders and many people depend on the strength of his character. He knows I am equally capable as a leader, and can share the load when he needs me to, and he trusts me to lead our family well. I love that. It's a sacred exchange between us, done without words. With one look into his eyes, I'll know my love needs me to carry his load. I can handle it and that is what makes me a badass... not fighting his leadership but letting him lead because I want him to and because I am secure in his knowing I am able and ready to step into leadership when he needs me to.

Honoring a good man is letting him do his job, loving him when the world kicks his ass, pointing him to God and other good men when he needs wisdom and staying the hell out of the rest. This secret sauce only works with a good man that truly leads and protects you from the storm, though, so keep your eyes wide open. Only a prepared woman will be able to distinguish the difference between a good man in a state of rest and a passive man that won't lead or take responsibility for protecting and providing for his family. Yes, good men are hard to find but they are easy to identify if you watch how they lead.

A Good Man Competes and Provides

Men are designed to compete. It is one of the things that motivates them to protect and provide. Men measure everything, and they constantly keep score. Most of the time when they are quiet they are competing in their minds in one form or another. This is also why when they sleep with a woman they call it a 'score'. (I am not suggesting that a man use a woman to 'score'; that is a dishonorable misuse of power and no different than when a women sleeps with a guy for the wrong reasons.)

Competing is the way they're wired, their basic nature. A man's need to compete is good...so let him compete! It's another driving force that makes him the very man we have imagined him to be. A good man keeps score lots of ways: with his beautiful wife, his well-behaved children, his nice home, his amazing career, and even how he serves his community. They are all points on the scoreboard of life. He is competing to be the best. A good man hungers to win, and he measures himself against other good men.

In fact, another great way to quickly identify a passive, weak or unprepared man is to see how he competes against other good men. A good man finds it enjoyable to see what other good men have accomplished because they want to compete against skilled opponents. He competes for the reward of providing, so when he wins big against a good opponent, this usually means you are about to reap the rewards in an abundant, rich way, like maybe your lifestyle gets kicked up a notch. I have no problem benefiting from being married to a competitive guy that wants to compete against even greater opponents! It's the difference between winning a baseball game against some kids in your neighborhood vs. pitching a no-hitter in the major leagues. I mean it's cute that he would play with kids...but it's life-changing and hot if he pitches for the Giants! I'm cool with being the wife of a major leaguer. Frankly, I'm competitive too so it means I win, as well.

Michael had such a crappy start in life with an alcoholic father, but his dad did teach him to work hard. Michael had a natural desire to compete in the 'big leagues' with men but fell into a life of crime in his younger years. When Michael sobered up, he made a very clear decision to win at life and to inspire others to push past their fears and not be defined by their pasts, either. Michael needed good men to learn from and compete against to prove himself well in this world and eventually inspire others.

We had just founded Crossing the Jordan and Michael heard that the CEO of the Chevron Oilstop was a local businessman in our community. Michael walked right into his office one day, unannounced, and said, "Hi, I'm Michael Bryant, I am a CEO and don't know how to be a good one. All I know is if I want to be successful, I need to hang out with successful men and learn. Will you be my mentor?"

That was seven years ago. Larry is still one of Michael's dearest friends to this day and Michael still runs tough decisions by him. During those early of our organization days we only brought in $50 a day. This year, we will do $3 million in sales. We started with only $500 in cash. The spirit of competition motivates Michael, and his love for people is what drives him to push further.

Since it takes money to impact as many lives as Crossing the Jordan has, and making money is a competitive game, Michael gets to win. We intend to make many more millions...unapologetically...because we know if we create a competitive environment for those that seek to change their lives, it keeps the bar high, and everyone wins.

In the scoreboard of life being a pilot is also a nice win, so Michael just became a licensed private pilot. So he is a CEO, a pilot, also a hiker, and a bodybuilder. Why? Because everything is about the next adventure. A selfish woman would see those interests as taking time away from his family, but I understand his need for adventure, I nurture it, in fact I cheer him on...because, girl, that fire in him has him providing the kind of life I only dreamed of.

I got this text from Michael the other day: *Be ready at five. I'm taking you on a date. Emma is taking the kids.*

I got ready, got in the car and assumed we were headed to the airport. He got on the freeway going the other way and I said, "We're driving? What?! Why aren't we flying to Napa?"

I caught myself and slapped my hand over my guilty grin, knowing that sounded bad. He smiled and wagged his finger me, "Be careful. Don't get too spoiled."

One could assume a few things from this interaction: either I'm a snooty spoiled b**ch and how can we run a nonprofit and afford a plane?! Or, I'm a woman that finally figured out what she wanted and went for it: I found a good competitive man who learned how to compete in the big leagues, who found high value men to learn from whom are now his friends, and they have planes we can use.

If all this talk about being competitive seems shallow or maybe just materialistic, just stop it, already. Of course we want a good life with nice things. Yes, we can be content with what we have—and still strive for more. There are always newer or bigger dreams to aim for. I want to see the world and experience some 'finer things' in life so I write books or train people or create quality content online for people to learn and improve their lives. As a result of sowing that good seed, I get to experience abundance and blessings and these over-the-top-experiences that I often have to pinch myself over. I won't let my past handicap me, and we only have one life, so I am going to make the rest of my life the best of my life. You can be kind, loving, generous... and hugely successful. Money and success aren't evil, people's choices with them are. It takes money to impact the world for good. We must be givers, not takers, but it takes having money in order to give it. A competitive man married to good woman can make the greatest impact! That's just the way it is, and there isn't a damn thing wrong with it.

When a man stops competing, he starts dying inside.

Often, good men don't care as much about the money they get from winning, they mostly just care about the win itself and the impact on their family and the world that it can result in. Because it's in their DNA to compete, the amounts they win can sometimes only be for the purpose of keeping score. Michael could care less about the actual income from deals he makes; it goes to the nonprofit and he hands me his paycheck. I have to make him spend money on himself most of the time. Since a good man competes for the sake of provision for his family, community or country, men often measure their true success by the impact it makes: it's what feeds a man's soul, gives him purpose, gives him his sense of identity and his place in society. Not competing can leave a man bereft of confidence, self-esteem, and a sense of purpose, ultimately leading into depression or even an early death.

You want a competitive man; you want a man that measures. If he measures in a way that provides for you and fulfills his sense of adventure, then he is competing the right way. He will be fulfill his purpose and you, my dear sister, will be the beneficiary of a life well spent. Don't resist; insist!

A Good Man has a Huge Ego

What?! I know. I've spent days thinking of different ways to title this section. I wanted to give you a spoonful of sugar to help the medicine go down, but I won't. This is good stuff and we can handle it, sugar or no. We're big girls and we should already have our big (sexy) girls' panties on.

The definition of ego for our purposes is: a person's sense of self-esteem, self-importance, or personal identity.

Synonyms: self-esteem, self-importance, self-worth, self-respect, self-image, self-confidence.

What really is an ego and what is it not? To put it simply, it's a person's sense of self, how people see themselves. It is not bad or good or your friend or your foe. The word ego itself has developed over time to have a negative connotation, usually associated with arrogance, too much pride, or empty boasting.

But if you look at the true definition and synonyms you could make the argument that it is good—even crucially important—especially for men. We tend to measure an ego because of the way we have been trained to look out for it, and so often misunderstand its true role in helping us choose a lifetime mate. Let's agree, that by definition, ego is not bad and not our enemy.

Further definitions:

Self-esteem: the confidence in one's own worth or abilities; self-respect.

Self-importance: an exaggerated sense of one's own value or importance.

Self-respect: pride and confidence in oneself; a feeling that one is behaving with honor and dignity.

As you can see by these definitions, a man must not be judged by his ego but by the content of his character. Self-esteem is necessary to lead, whereas self-importance can hinder your ability to lead well, if at all. Can we agree that subduing our egos do not make us better women or men? In fact, expressing our egos without words is quite powerful, if our sense of self is grounded in honor, dignity, pride, confidence, and our ability to contribute.

So, a man having an ego does not make him a raging narcissist. If a man harnesses his ego appropriately, it gives him a competitive advantage, since a man measures everything and the first thing he measures on another man is the size of his ego. A good man won't even compete with another man that has an inflated ego of too much self-importance. That is arrogance, which we often misinterpret as a big ego, and it's not worth the effort of a good man. He's already won by not giving an arrogant man his time or energy.

Here goes: *Stroking the ego is the best way to get and/or keep a good man.* Truly. Further, we should actively be looking for the man with the biggest ego! The only concern or exception would be if you yourself are not yet prepared for a man by mastering the four areas: sisterhood, self-possession, service and sex…because if you haven't then you are in SERIOUS DANGER of stroking the wrong type of ego.

Definition of arrogance: having or revealing an exaggerated sense of one's own importance or abilities

Synonyms: haughty, conceited, self-important, superior, over-bearing, pompous, immodest, big-headed

Since this is what our culture is misunderstanding, we are warning our women to not 'feed his ego'. As a result, not only are we not feeding his ego, we have taken it to the extreme and trained ourselves as women to fight against the ego, causing further damage.

But guess how a man responds when you fight his ego? *He translates it as competition and he is driven even more to win.* A good man will even fight you if you compete with him. This is the reason for some of our conflict in the workplace with men. He won't fight dishonorably but he will fight. Remember, I didn't make the rules. The rules are designed to keep us safe, fed, clothed and housed. Our brains are programed for our survival. Men are designed for our protection and to help us survive. In fact, when they accomplish this mission, it is when they experience the greatest reward, the self-respect and sense of worth they are craving. Why would we try to take that from them?

Ask a man that has lost his way. I dare you to dig deep, past the arrogance and self-importance, past the thinking this lost man is suffering because he isn't expressing his emotions enough, past the interpretation that he's lost because our society needs to re-define masculinity or neutralize the gender roles, and really ask a man *why?*

Ask men that are crushed over their life choices. Men that are jobless, depressed, divorced, have abused women, become gang members or are in prison. I have asked. If we get quiet enough and close enough—once we shut off the voices of our own agendas and we listen, and I mean listen to their words and the actions behind their pain—you will almost always get the same answer: *they failed at protecting and providing for their families.*

The image they created in their minds as a boy, that they would leap tall buildings in a single bound, rescue their beauty and live great adventures, was the one they failed at. They failed at fulfilling their own dreams. Tragically, our own society has really start-ed to demonize his dreams and deride his masculinity. It's hard to become a good man these days. Boys are being pressured out of their superman dreams, told that dodgeball is violent and toy guns will turn him into a killer. We send them off into a compet-itive world equipped with no skills to compete with and no clue how to find a good mate. We've just done things so backwards, for boys. We strip our boys of their armor (ego), take away their weapons (competition) then send them out into a cruel, compet-itive, dangerous battlefield (world) and hope they will be victori-ous. It's a wonder they can even survive!

Why are we so afraid of the ego? Great leaders have big egos. If they didn't, they wouldn't have the motivation and endurance to be the best. Why minimize the kind of character it takes to be the best? Do you know how hard it is to be the very best at some-thing? It takes guts, discipline, training, pain, delayed gratifica-tion, risk of failure, blind faith, determination and perseverance.

Michael has an ego the size of Texas. The level of confidence he walks in feels like a tornado blowing through town sometimes. Our corporate offices are in a 22,000 sq. ft., 3-story building and you know when he's in the building. Every employee and intern can tell me where he is, when he arrived or if he has left.

It's quite entertaining to me. We started in our garage together. I used to dream of the day that our offices were on opposite ends of a building and that is exactly where there are today—each of our offices as far apart from one another as possible. I chuckle when I hear the sigh of one of his assistants or team members. People know he is in the building, not because he treats them poorly, but because he has trained them to be on their toes, with their game faces on, always giving their utmost in excellence. Michael isn't easy to work for and I love that about him. He's not cruel or abusive in any way, but he pushes his team out of their comfort zones, always challenging them, encouraging them to step up their game and rise to the next level in a spirit of service. It takes big cojones to pull that off. A passive man couldn't, he'd be too selfish. Passive people don't want to be uncomfortable, so they continue to allow what should be stopped challenged or changed, taking the path of least resistance, the path needing the least protection. We must care about the people we've been entrusted us to lead, to call them up to their God-given gifts.

Recently, I was at a training and a man said, 'It takes a powerful woman to manage a man with a big ego.' It's true because you can't play the victim to a confident leader, he won't tolerate it. You can allow yourself to be weak during times of legitimate trouble because a strong man won't let you stay in your misery, and that's a good thing. A high value man with a high level of self-respect won't settle for mediocrity with anyone in his life, so it takes one hell of a woman to walk boldly and equally beside a man that knows what he wants. She has to hold that kind of strong space with him, be confident in who she is and go after life with him. Be that kind of girl and you will attract a man that oozes self-worth and defies insecurity. It takes a special kind of woman to hang on to a guy like this, so prepare yourself for him. That big ego can take you anywhere you want to go. Don't run from that kind of man, run towards him and then with him.

A Good Man Serves

As a young woman, the idea of a man serving me looked like breakfast in bed or a bedroom scattered with rose petals. I never really envisioned much beyond that. Envisioning a man encouraging me to chase my dreams? Nowadays, I sure can, that's easy. I can picture that in my mind all day long. He would say things like *Get it girl, you can do it*, or *I've got your back, just go for it*. A man like that might cook dinner for me after a late night at work, partner with me to watch the kids or rub my back when I'm sore. That's awesome and it is a part of what a good man does.

When Michael and I met, I shared excitedly about my dream of starting a nonprofit. The nonprofit would be a social enterprise that served women and children that struggled the way I had with Chelsea, my oldest, before I met Michael. I would describe every detail and he would listen intently. He'd invite me to talk about it, morning, noon and night, hearing the hunger in my heart to make an impact in the world and make sense of what I had gone through. When I would try to tell *others* that I felt strongly about starting a nonprofit, you could just sense the rolling of their eyes inside their heads. A dream like that seemed a little too big of a vision than people could get on board with, from a woman that had ruined her life, or so it seemed.

Afterwards, Michael would read the disappointment in my face after these encounters, and he could sense me allowing my dream to begin to die, so he would stoke the fire with his constant curiosity and questions. I had tried to open a women's home on my own, before we met, but kept failing. Michael breathed hope back into my vision instead of judging me for being tired of trying and failing. In fact, he took my dream and adopted it as his own purpose. If you asked Michael even today, he will tell you, "I decided to lay down my dreams to serve hers and as a result, God blessed me more than I could ever have imagined." He will tell you that as he became a servant to my vision and it unfolded, God gave him his.

Michael pushed me every day to take action on what I felt called to do. He encouraged me to go for it. When the fire inside of me burned bright, it was like everywhere I went I was running into women that were hurting and wanting a new way of life, so I would minister to them. In no time at all, we were getting known for helping those in need. We didn't have our nonprofit yet and not one extra dollar to make it all happen, but Michael and I just started to serve together, in the first months of us being together. People started to call us about women in trouble who had children and we started to take them into our home, love on them and then have to find them programs outside of our area (because there were none locally, which ticked me off).

Michael served right alongside me. When I look back on those days, I got the lion's share of the glory for the vision I had been given. He never said a word about that. He rarely was acknowledged for his efforts at all during that season of our lives. Originally, I started the nonprofit with a few women that I chose for all the wrong reasons, thinking having prominent women associated with us would somehow be insurance against any judgment of my past. Unfortunately, those women were the very ones that judged me. When we first started the nonprofit and began to fundraise, Michael was the first to arrive and last to leave at all the functions, carrying the brunt of the behind-the-scenes-work. I was a rookie and I had no idea what I was doing. I was also so distracted by the women that were hurting me, falling victim to some of my old fears, that I didn't fully appreciate his efforts at the time. Michael didn't complain. He just kept cheering me on.

Those early days of Crossing the Jordan were all-consuming. Starting the nonprofit, opening our first store and then finally opening the first women and children's home took every ounce of courage and fortitude I could muster. When that first Board of women finally resigned, I found myself standing there alone until I opened my eyes to realize Michael was by my side, and had been the whole time. He never even mentioned that he had consciously set aside his dreams for mine. He trusted God to take care of them, in time.

I did cry myself to sleep a few times over the betrayal of those women I first trusted with my dream, because I had longed for a sisterhood for so long that seemed so difficult to find. I knew that I could make an impact on so many lives and I was determined that my past would mean something because I had been selfish for long enough. Looking back on that season with those ladies, I realized I was wrong to expect that from them. I had asked those women to engage with me in a battle they were not equipped for. Michael and I were battle-ready because of where we had been and how God had trained us through our suffering and it wasn't realistic to ask these women to go to the types of dark places we had to go. Michael had tried to warn me, but I was living out my insecurities a lot in those early days and didn't listen, and when that Board of women left I continued to fight off the bitter thoughts: *You can't trust women. They will just hurt you.* I started to build a wall around myself, hindering myself from pursuing my vision. Why was it all so damn hard? Why did it seem impossible to step into my purpose? Why was there so much resistance? We were rolling pennies to make rent. We had trusted God and walked away from our good paying jobs. It went against everything competitive in both of us, but we knew it was time and we had the courage to jump when God said jump. We were walking door to door with our children putting flyers on doors asking the community to donate their unwanted items to a store that wasn't open for a home for women and children we didn't have yet. It was crazy. All of it.

One evening, Michael opened the front door to find me sobbing on the porch uncontrollably. "I can't do it honey. I'm sorry I dragged you into all of this. It's too much. I'm just a dreamer, that's all and I just don't know when to stop. I'm so sorry I did this to our family. It's too much pressure."

Michael just stood there in the doorway calmly, leaning on the door frame, arms crossed watching me try to give up on my dream. He didn't bend down to comfort or rescue me in any way, although I could see in his eyes he wanted to…but he knew what I was capable of and he had to call me up to my better self, where I hungered to be.

"Honey look at me. Stand up and look at me," he said. I rose to him slowly. He wiped my eyes. "This is the moment in time that most people give up. This is the exact moment that most people break and give in and then never accomplish what they set out to do. If it was easy, everyone would be doing it. You can't quit. There are too many women out there that need you to not give up. They are waiting for you and counting on you to help them. I won't do it for you, but I will do it with you."

I was never the same after that night. He held me but only for a moment. Michael wanted me to decide, apart from him, what I was willing to sacrifice for others. He knew what kind of woman I would have to become to do what I dared to do. I will never forget that day. It is etched into my soul and in times of trouble, I anchor onto the decision I made that night. He was right: most people give up when it gets too hard and never serve out their purpose or become the person they are meant to be.

The next morning, I woke up to Michael sitting in the truck with the kids, waiting for me with a cup of coffee for me in his hand. It was 6am. We had put flyers out in the neighborhood a few days before with a note saying we would pick up the donations early that morning. We had been getting very little results, which was one of the reasons I was so disheartened and questioning if we were headed in the right direction. We had been blindly stepping out in faith, always expecting the best but seemingly only getting the worst in responses.

Michael and the kids were always so sweet on pick up day, always excited about the adventure, but this day? This day my husband knew I needed a miracle. We stopped our old beat up truck on the corner before the street with the flyers. Michael prayed, "God, we need a miracle. My baby needs you to show up right now and show her we are doing what You want us to do."

We turned the corner—and burst out in happy tears. Both sides of the streets were lined with so many bags and donations, it was as if the whole neighborhood had turned out to cheer us on. We just stared at each other, mouths hanging open, tears rolling down our smiling cheeks, in awe of God's grace. All four of us hopped out of the truck with more joy than we could contain. Our children were changed that day. Our cup had runneth over. As we took trip after trip back and forth to pick it all up, we knew we could withstand anything after this.

That was over seven years ago. Crossing the Jordan serves and operates three residential facilities with over 80 residents, including their children. The nonprofit is a multimillion-dollar social enterprise with six retail stores, a recycling export operation, and a moving and storage company experiencing explosive growth. The nonprofit does not receive one government dollar and is fully funded through the industries we created out of just $500.

A good man serves. He will come alongside your dreams and love you all the way to the top. You will have some bad days. We fought during some of those moments. Every good man won't be perfectly romantic and some of the romantic men won't be tough enough with you. You can count on it getting messy and you can rest assured that you will feel at times like you will never find a man like I did with Michael. Those men are rare, but they are out there and worth waiting for. Be watchful. A good man's service may come in different varieties and styles so pay attention and give him a chance to shine. A good man will always find a way to serve the woman he loves.

A Good Man Honors Your Good Men

I was almost done writing this book and out of nowhere Michael turns to me and says, "I can't believe I keep forgetting to talk to you about the most important sign if a man is a good man."

"What do you mean?"

"We forgot the most important one. The biggest and earliest red flag that a man is not prepared yet and the best sign to look for that he is. You have got to train women to look for this one."

"Tell me already, I'm dying!"

"A good man will honor and intentionally draw close to the good men in a woman's life that she honors," Michael explained.

It was a bit of an 'aha!' moment. I knew this, but I had not utilized it as a resource until my good man pointed it out to me. Michael honored my father and other good men I loved and had initiated a relationship with them. To this day, he is constantly nurturing the relationships. Michael knew that by reaching out to my male family and friends, most importantly the honorable men in such a respectful way, was a sign that he was a good man and worthy of my hand in marriage. Until Michael explained it that way I had no idea just how intentional he had been about it. Yes, it came naturally to him because he enjoyed the company of good men, but he was also aware it was a strategy to get the girl. I loved that.

When I began to ponder how this impacts a relationship, I realized that Michael is the ONLY man that went after the relationships of the good men I cared for and respected most. I had a few male friends in my life, like Jack, the one who told me to always be as hot as the mistress would be. I remembered that Michael insisted the four of us, Jack, his wife Michelle (my friend of 20 years), and Michael and I go out to dinner, so he could meet Jack. Wow, now that was HOT!

Michael showed interest in the men that I spoke highly of. Michael even nurtured the fond memories I had of my grandfather, once a professional boxer in New York, who had passed away so many years before. My grandfather's dying words to me were that I marry a good man. Michael adored the fact that my grandfather, whom he never met, had his dying wish come true through him. As for any other men or business mentors that supported me through my transformation, Michael went out of his way to engage with them—even my former Federal Parole Officer that I stayed in contact with.

I am in awe as I write this because I had no idea that Michael had a strategy to make me his wife until he shared these strategies with me, and now I can share them with you. I knew my strategies...and obviously, he must have had some...but I guess I just didn't think how intentional he was about executing them. I am flooded now with sweet memories of how he continues to actively pursue the good men in my life. I feel safe and cherished because of it.

The bad men in my life did the exact opposite. Unqualified, unprepared, or bad men run from good men and work like hell to manipulate us to keep us away from good men, and they work hard to isolate us from our family, as well. Even the ones that might appear to be the good guy at first, in time, cannot hold the space of good men because, by comparison, they are exposed quite quickly for who they truly are. Insecure or bad men must avoid the exposure of their character at all costs.

A good man runs toward the good men; not just as a strategy but because they truly value the benefits of association with them. After Michael told me this, it's like he pulled the curtain back on one key aspect of our men's program. He clearly teaches these strategies to the good men that graduate. As I thought over the six married couples (graduates) we walked closely with through courtship, all the men deeply honor Michael and they each intentionally have pursued the good men in their wives' lives. It's like their own code of conduct that seals the deal with a good woman.

We have a very strong and close tribe at Crossing the Jordan. Occasionally, one of the women will date a very unprepared guy. The coolest part of an accountable community is that an immature man (or shall we say, boy) usually doesn't last more than a few weeks around us. Our tribe is huge, and these women have close relationships with their 'brothers' in the tribe. So, at a barbecue or other group activity, once the bad man realizes he is among an army of good men, he is out of there so fast sometimes it's comical. The benefit of trusting those in your community is that it weeds out those that we might be fooled by, saving women time and heartache. The women in my tribe aren't crushed, either, because they have learned the benefits of operating this way, as they are in the process of becoming good, solid women. They realize it's the quickest way to vet a man——get him in a crowd of people you honor and see how he handles it. If he 'can't' and comes up with a million lame excuses why he can't, dump him immediately. Period. Don't 'co' his excuses and don't get trapped by his manipulation. Don't hide your head in the sand because if you do, it just reveals that you have some more work to do, which is ok. It's not a 'lose' if the bad man leaves you because you just saved yourself years, if not a lifetime, of suffering. It's a win.

A good man will honor and hold you in high regard as well as the good men you hold dear. Expect it, and watch for it, and make sure he does. It's the best and fastest way to discover what kind of man he really is.

A Good Man Carries Your Baggage

I've noticed that we seem to approach good men one of two ways: either we feel we are entitled to them or we think we can't have them because of the baggage we carry. Let's talk about our 'baggage' in relation to how a good man handles it.

As I began to live out of forgiveness and become a good woman, I still had this little anxiety tucked away in me about how a good man would deal with my past. I could sense I was becoming quite a catch but there was this hesitation inside of me when I imagined having to explain the 'baggage' of my past I would be carrying into the relationship. I didn't call it baggage because I knew enough by now that it wasn't appealing for anyone to relate to it that way, but, as I began to believe I was worthy of a good man and ready for him, I cringed when I pictured explaining the horrible things I had done.

Thankfully Michael and I had similar pasts, so when we met it was easy to explain mine, but still, he had been become a good man and I was terrified he wouldn't want to take on my wreckage. My teenager Chelsea was pissed off at the world at that time, for what had happened between her father and I, and dealing with that was all-consuming for me right around the time I met Michael. I had left her from age 2 – 8 years old while I was in prison, and she was bitter. Chelsea and I fought constantly. However, right in the throes of her rebellion and in such a short amount of time, I noticed she began to trust Michael in unexpected ways. He never judged her—while I seemed to never stop. It was an intense time in her upbringing and as incident after incident happened, I grew fearful it would be too much for any man to handle.

One day, Michael announced that he was taking Chelsea and me to Napa. He wouldn't explain, and I was told not to ask. We pulled up to a private airport even though we didn't have the money to fly on a private plane. We walked in to the Napa Airport and they were expecting us. Chelsea had once told Michael she had wanted to learn how to fly and maybe be a pilot someday, so Michael had arranged for flying lessons for her! Soon I was watching Chelsea up in an airplane with her instructor, soaring through the skies.

I stood there in awe of Michael as I watched him looking up at the sky. I had been with such bad men, it seemed unreal that anyone would do this for my child…would do this for ME. I stood there speechless. I looked at him and said, pathetically, "Thank you so much for all you've done. Neither of us deserve this."

Ouch. That came out of my mouth. I was embarrassed to reveal thoughts of such low self-worth.

Michael looked down at me, eyes watering, hurt, as if I was trying to steal something special from him. "Don't you get it? I am the blessed one. I get to do this. The honor is mine."

I finally understood at that moment that my baggage was never his burden. He loved me with all that I came with: my struggles, my fears, my finances, my unwanted weight, my broken-down car, my insecurities and my heartache. He never once related to it as baggage, as I did, and he never mentioned the mistakes I had made to get there. He thought of it in terms of helping me to unpack it all and let it go. It was almost rude and selfish of me to try to carry my baggage alone, to assume he saw what I brought into the relationship as something he didn't want to help me get through.

A good man's heart is to serve you. A good man will love you with all that you bring with you and he will be patient as you unpack all the junk you need to let go of. Even if he doesn't carry it perfectly, a good man won't hold it against you. You will be tempted to carry it alone when times are tough, but don't. A good man can handle it. Let him.

A Good Man Waits

What I am about to tell you will either irritate you or move a part of your heart that you've longed to treasure and hold sacred. We live in a culture where delayed gratification is a lost art and living on-demand is today's standard. Waiting for a good man seems ridiculous and foolish to those of us swimming in a sea of settling and compromise.

As we discover who a good man is and what he does, we must learn to develop the greatest tool we have as a woman—making him wait. There is an art to making him wait…and not just for sex. When we discuss the subject of waiting, there's more. We will discuss sex more thoroughly in coming chapters but I will take a little time here to discuss courting.

I believe in courting. Courting is developing a relationship with someone with the intent of learning if they are compatible for marriage or not, without the complexity of physical and sexual intimacy clouding the relationship. Courting is the vital discovery phase.

Let me remind you that I did sleep around as a young woman and I will NOT be religious and judgmental about the subject. I'm a believer, yes, but in no way am I preaching at you to stay pure. I am only discussing this for the purpose of producing results, because we are on a mission to find and keep a good man. (Married women: clearly, you are having sex, so just hang in there while we discuss this really quick.)

The point is to test a good man's patience during the discovery phase. Once you're a qualified and prepared woman yourself, looking for a good man, understand that *making a man wait is the single best way to discover what kind of man he really is.*

I remember when Michael and I had our first big fight. I was a mess. I hadn't had my heart truly ache in a long while, so I freaked out when it hit me. Then this awful panicky fear of losing him washed over me and instead of talking about it, my survival instinct kicked in: I took flight. I jumped in the car and drove off trying to hide my tears.

He called my cell phone and asked, "Where are you going?"

I tried to hide my sobbing and answered, "I can't do this. I'm sorry. This is too hard." I hung up and turned my phone off. I knew Michael didn't like drama and he didn't play games, so I assumed it was just over. I had blown it. There was another woman he'd been interested in at the time we met so I just assumed he would go to her and pick up where he left off since we hadn't been together long. It's silly but I remember thinking: *You did it, Dana. It's over. Now get yourself together. Do not let anyone see you this way again. You cannot fall apart.*

No man had ever chased after me. Not in my entire life. I had been with cheaters, abusers and a few actually nice guys, but I just wasn't the type of woman that was chased after, I assumed, and it always stung me when I would watch a movie about or hear that a woman I knew was being chased. It always served as an awful reminder of how little others thought of me, or how little I thought of myself. I mean I didn't look bad, and men wanted me…there was plenty of make-up sex and dramatic re-unions…but no man had ever made the effort to really fight for me in the way that it mattered. It gnawed at my self-worth and hurt to think about.

I thought I was over that kind of insecure sensitivity by the time I met Michael. As I drove towards home with tears streaming down my face I had a talk with myself. *Stop this behavior, Dana, you are not who you used to be. You've done the hard work. You are worthy of being chased. Michael was wrong, and it's ok. Maybe he's not the One. You ARE worth waiting for. If Michael isn't willing to fight for you and wait for you to fully heal then he's not the right guy. Wait for the good guy, the one you've been preparing for.*

My little conversation didn't help the pain, though. I was feeling rejected and my wounds were still bleeding. I do remember that my little pep talk reminded me of what I was willing to wait for: a good man, my good man. I turned my phone back on and my heart sunk further: Michael hadn't called. Ouch. *Here we go again.* Rejection just hurts the worst.

You're ready, Dana. You know what you want, and you can't ever settle again. The good thoughts were hard to focus on, but I kept at it, because I could sense I was breaking a pattern. I had been taking time to heal, get ready and prepare myself to create the life I had always wanted the past few years, and I didn't need a man. I only wanted a good one.

Ding dong. My heart racing, I opened the door—it was Michael!

He reached for my hand and gently pulled me out onto the porch with him. "I'm not quite sure what is going on here, but I'm not the guy you push away or turn your phone off, on."

Wait…oh God, is this really happening?

"Dana, I will wait for you. However long it takes to get you through your pain, I will wait."

Ohhhh…my. I was healed—supernaturally—that night. I can't explain it well, but it was a precious gift from God. The fear just evaporated off me. It was as if my willingness to wait was the secret catalyst I needed to free myself of all the years of compromise, unreadiness and unwillingness (to do the hard work) that had robbed me of the kind of love I had dreamed of, and all of it built up to this one moment, when my life shifted miraculously as the longing of my heart was answered. *He came after me! He didn't just call or wait until tomorrow. Michael chased after ME*

"I can't imagine my life without you," he said, as he held me tenderly and let me cry out loud. He sensed this moment was way bigger than our silly little fight. "Dana, I will always come after you and I will never let you get away."

I could barely breathe when he softly kissed the top of my head and whispered, "I've been waiting for you, too."

A good man waits. Expect him to.

Chapter 6

What A Good Woman Does

Becoming the Butterfly

Transformation, by nature, is a violent process. Imagine what a caterpillar goes through to become a butterfly. I know we haven't really thought about that since kindergarten but think about transformation at a cellular level. The process didn't happen overnight, and once complete, the caterpillar looks absolutely nothing like the butterfly, it's completely unrecognizable. It went from an ugly bug into a flying colorful beauty. The butterfly's freedom to fly came with great discomfort.

Willingness to transform our lives manifests when we have come to the end of ourselves, acknowledging that our current reality isn't working. On a rare occasion we notice what's wrong before there are devastating consequences, and we take the necessary steps to shift. Most often, we are reactive beings, only willing to change when we have experienced sufficient pain and suffering. Where are you right now? Are you ready to go through the process of transformation at a 'cellular level?' Or are you tinkering around, still looking for a quick fix that *feels* like change?

True change, like the butterfly, does not happen within the confines of comfort. Quick fixes are literally a waste of time. You're not getting any younger and *time* is of the essence. I'm saying this because what we are about to discuss may feel like violent change, but let's not be ruled by our emotions. Instead let the feeling sit in your body, acknowledge it, then let it pass through you on out. We might have to sacrifice some stuff to get what we want, but we're grownups and we can admit it takes humility to live excellently.

We've already been made to feel comfortable, anyway...we've been catered to, fed lies, and been told things that get us excited and temporarily empowered with a bunch of 'tools' that sound like they will work but don't really. No, I'm not gonna do that to you. This tool belt I am setting you up with has tools that actually work—tools that double as effective weapons against the lies out there that might steal your family and your dreams. Now that will be badass.

There are real and present threats to living out your dreams, out there. We will address some you maybe haven't thought of. Now that we know what a man wants and who a good man is, we are ready to learn what a good woman *does*. We will discuss our own personal growth in these chapters. We will identify how a good woman interacts in the relationship, how we show up and when to shut up. (Yeah, we can be our own worst enemy sometimes.)

I'll keep reminding you to stay curious. This is about getting qualified and prepared.

A Good Woman Manages the Relationship

I figured we should start with the fun, empowering stuff. That's right—*we are the official relationship managers.* When I figured this out, it made so much sense. When it comes to relationships, women are the architects and men are the builders. You want to talk about feminine power? Oh boy, when I got a handle on this truth, everything changed in our house.

You mean I don't have to wait around for him to change? The success of our marriage isn't based on how he behaves? How can this be? How can he be the 'leader' and I be the manager? It doesn't make sense!

Yes, it does!

Remember, a man wants a battle to fight, a beauty to rescue and an adventure to live. If you get this and understand that men have simple needs—love, sex, family and your wisdom and intuition—is it hard to create plans for him to build that kind of life? If you are truly the complex, creative, emotional creature we all know you are, why can't you step in as the 'architect' you're designed to be and give him the 'plans' that he needs to 'build' the life that you both always wanted?

Draw up the blueprints; he'll build the dream. I'm not saying you won't build too, of course, it's life, and you must get up every morning and do *your* part. What I am saying is that you are the one in charge of the plans and he *wants* to be the builder. It's in his DNA. The art to being the architect is to communicate the plans in such a way that honors his masculinity without coming across as superior. (In fact, you don't need to ever call yourself an 'architect', I mean, a good man won't really care, and he'll agree to what you're saying if you communicate respectfully and not contentiously. It's all about the delivery.)

The life I have today is a direct result of the vision I had and the marriage I have today is the direct result of the 'architectural plans' I learned to create. It takes vision for both so if you are unclear about your vision, how can you make plans? If you don't have a clear vision yet, just stay with me, we will work on that later.

I am naturally a visionary. The issue in my youth was that I never took the time to be the architect of that vision and write it down. Until then, my vision was just a daydream. I was just fantasizing, like most of us do…but once the plans are put to paper it really starts getting exciting. All that was missing from me having the relationship I always wanted was to draw up the plans, find a good man and let him build! Once I understood that, girl, you'd better believe I started drawing!

When we started Crossing the Jordan, we only had one thrift store in a bad part of town. We had to operate our offices from there, as well. Then, when we grew and moved our offices to our warehouse, it still wasn't where I wanted our offices to be. The warehouse had rats and it just felt unprofessional and it was kind of gross and it just…was NOT a part of my vision. I didn't like having to walk past a mountain of recycled garbage every day to get to my office or for our team to operate this way. So, *in the spirit of excellence* (which we train our Crossing the Jordan residents to live by), I dreamed of having our offices in a large, beautiful building, with a corner office for myself, overlooking downtown. I began to focus on and plan for that dream, meditating on it and praying for it regularly.

I had been eyeing this old building on the corner of our main street that'd been empty for years. It was a diamond in the rough: kind of shabby, covered in a bad paint job, but with gorgeous architecture. It was right in the heart of downtown across from the Santa Rosa mall, with 3 floors, over 22,000 square feet, and a retail space on the ground floor. I had dreamed of developing our brand to include a designer just-like-new resale clothing store and this building fit perfectly with that vision. I began to draw up the plans in my mind (and heart) a good six months before the day I finally shared it with Michael.

One afternoon we happened to drive by and stop at the light. I looked up at the building and said, "Someday that building is going to be ours. That corner office will be mine, and the Boutique would be beautiful on the bottom floor. Best of all, it will be a beacon of light in our city for people hoping for change."

We wanted our brand to represent the challenge and adventure of a new life and if we could revitalize this giant building right in the middle of our city, it would be like a metaphor of that change, and a stake in the ground for God's message of hope for those hurting.

"That would be something amazing, wouldn't it?" Michael answered. "Write down the number. Let's call and see what happens."

Michael made the call, and by the next morning we were in a meeting with the property manager and then moved in to the ground floor 30 days later. We remodeled the building with my vision in mind (and the owner's money) within 6 months. We moved our corporate offices and classrooms in by end of the year. I sit here writing today in that revitalized, gorgeous building, with a corner view to the dream I dared to plan and act on. But I couldn't have done it alone: I needed a builder and Michael stepped in, took the plans and began to build (made it happen). He got on board with my vision, and as the builder, immediately started to implement the plans.

This same scenario has played out in every aspect of our relationship. For example, Michael is a workaholic and he would never slow down. I planned for him to *want* to slow down and rest regularly since our life flows better when he has time to get restored. Instead of nagging him to be home more often, I casually reminded him that I loved it when he took me to The Palace Hotel in San Francisco and that it's my favorite thing to do with him.

'I just love it when we have tea in the lobby together,' I'd say about every three months or so. 'It makes me feel cherished, like the most pampered woman in the world.'

Michael has now taken me there at least ten times, now. And you know what else he does? Like clockwork, after he's left me in the room for a while or I've gone out window shopping alone or with the kids, I'll get a call from him. "Come to the lobby. Let's have some tea together," he says. I can just see the smile on his face as he does this, every time, because I know the call is coming, and he knows I know he is going to make it, but it still never loses its fun and romance and the invitation is always as special as the first time.

I planned that whole scenario—and he built it into reality. Our vacations have consistently been smooth and without argument. To be best friends, not just business partners, i s so crucial. Having that intimate time together is vitally important. I plan it, share the vision with him about what the end result looks like and he makes it happen.

Michael builds what I plan because I *plan*. Even though he initiates more than ever now because he knows what I like, he loves being the one to bring the dream to life between us, he adores spoiling me in unique personal ways, and he wants to build a strong foundation to demonstrate for our children. I am careful to honor and appreciate him verbally, never belittle him or act superior, and always thank him when he follows through.

It takes humility to be a good architect. Yes, it takes vision, but also an awareness of what's *not* working and a willingness to be wrong in case we need to scrap the plans and resubmit new ones.

You are the manager, the architect and the responsible party in the development of the bond between you and your good man. Presence yourself in such a way that he *can't wait* to build a marriage and family with you that will stand the test of time.

A Good Woman Doesn't Bark

I can't wait to share this one with you. If you get this one down, you're seasoned architects, ready for the best of marriages. It might kill you at first, but it will turn any good man into the greatest of builders!

I have a loud mouth, I love to argue. (I always used to imagine myself at a trial in a courtroom when I was growing up.) I had no control over the tone of my voice, I had my default b**tch face down perfectly and considered *backing down* to be *giving up*. Since Michael was such a strong leader from day one, I took his need to compete as a personal challenge every time…and he responded accordingly.

A woman should never compete with a man in a relationship, not head on, anyways, and not in the way men fight other men. Not because we aren't competitors or we aren't capable of winning. We shouldn't compete with men only because *men don't know HOW to compete with women.* They get confused and start competing with us like we're men.

Women are more complex. We can adapt. But men just want to win. It's in their DNA because it's what drives them to provide and protect. When we compete with them, as a man—head on, barking back at them, showing them up or straight up in their face—they will fight back and bark back and do all manner of 'stupid' things.

I'm not suggesting that we don't get our way! I am suggesting that we stop trying to win by acting like a man. Yup, I said it. When we bark, yell, get in their face, call them names, assert our so-called power, show them who's boss, all that crap we seem so determined to do—that's a green light for them to respond back to us *like a man.* I am suggesting that we get our way by using the resource that we have naturally, our true source of feminine power—our managing skills—instead. *Don't bark; architect.* Design the outcome you desire.

Michael isn't a big sports fan. He'd rather fly a plane, backpack into the mountains, body build or drive a speedboat. I love to play basketball and softball. I play on our company co-ed team, but he'd *never* come to watch any games. Rude, right? It irritated me, so I called him out about it in front of other people. He still didn't come. Each week I found new ways to show him my disappointment and resentment about it. We were at a standstill until I realized it was because I was competing with him in front of other men about it. Even though I was genuinely hurt, that's not what I was communicating. He only saw my need to compete and try to assert *my* way in getting him there.

One day I was leaving for my game, all suited up, when Michael, my son, and his friend Brian pulled up. They looked in rush, so I asked, "Where are you going?"

The fact that I had my uniform on probably triggered us both. "I'm going to set up for tomorrow's event. Why?" He barked aggressively.

I felt the fight well up in me and then I heard my own training voice in my head. S*top competing!*

"Oh", I responded quickly, gently and with a smile. "Thank you so much for doing all that so I can go play ball."

Then I turned around and hopped cheerfully into my car. It wasn't even an act, I *felt* happy and excited because I hadn't lost my temper or dwelled on feeling hurt. Instead I just *decided* in that moment that competing wasn't working and chose to architect a new plan. I watched Michael in my side view mirror: he stood there for a half a second, taken aback by my grateful response. In addition, I was also grateful because I don't like to cook, and he had to plan to cook for 80 people the next day, so I *was* grateful I could just go play ball.

At the game later, I was right in the middle of a great play when I looked up and saw Michael there in the stands. Sarah, my friend at 1st base, looked at me and said, "Oh my gosh, Michael is here." She knew it had hurt me when he kept making excuses not to come.

Honestly, the moment I chose to not bark and instead, respond in love, I had a feeling he'd show up that night. I just *knew*, instinctively. He loved me, and he didn't like to compete with me. When we used to fight in the past, he would tell me that he didn't even know why he reacted the way he did sometimes. Michael is an intelligent man and even he couldn't pinpoint why he would have such a hard time not reacting to me this way. Later, when I learned why men are the way they are, it all made sense. He had responded to me as if I was a man, and that had hurt and upset me.

See, even smart men don't understand these complexities! Not in the moment, at least. So it takes women to manage the relationship. The funny thing though is that Michael knew I was studying masculinity and how men behave. He knew I was trying a new approach...*in that moment*...and he *still* was totally disarmed! He wasn't offended, arrogant, or embarrassed that I was 'using' what I had learned 'on him.' He didn't say, "Don't play games with me," or "You can't manipulate me to get me to your game." Nope. He was happy! I took off the pressure to compete that I had put on him. He was free to just be happy that I was happy. He drove to the game and freely cheered me on. He kissed me on top of the head when I scored. He smiled (quite sexily) from afar when I caught a ball. He didn't drown me in compliments because he knows I don't really like that too much. (I equate too many compliments with a man being needy: needy men aren't competitive and so they don't win big in life and I'm not into that.) That day I learned to manage the relationship, getting Michael to do what I wanted him to do, and he didn't mind at all because it honored him as a man.

A good woman doesn't bark, she architects. And her marriage thrives.

A Good Woman Doesn't Live in Hurt

Living in hurt demands payment. When women get hurt we tend to *stay* hurt—putting constant pressure on the person that hurt us. We assume if we were to 'get over' something too quickly, we wouldn't communicate to them how much it hurt us, right? Yeah…not really a good strategy. Trust me, they're over it most of the time anyway, and we're the only one that's miserable.

I lived in hurt like this in my marriage for quite some time. One time, when Michael and I were in the middle of one of only three major breakdowns in our marriage (it was a doozy) neither of us seemed willing to shift, and that's rare for us. I was coincidentally at the beginning of really diving deeply into the principles I am telling you about here, but somehow this issue was really a blind spot for me, so I believe God used this situation to make sure I understood what I was teaching. Sarah, our Director of Programs at Crossing the Jordan, shared something with me one day that stopped me in my tracks. As I sat there in her office crying my eyes out, shocked that Michael and I were unable to reconcile, Sarah stated quite unemotionally that she had learned to simply 'decide not to live in hurt.'

I wanted to flip out on her right there.

"OK, Sarah. I just won't be hurt." I retorted, rolling my eyes.

"Great," she responded cheerfully "That's what I do. I just *decide* I won't live from a place of hurt."

God, I love that woman, but in that moment I could feel myself just getting more hurt over how simple she made it sound. The mere fact that I was so upset at Sarah should've been a red flag, but I didn't pay attention.

It was hard enough to stop barking and competing, now I am supposed to never be hurt?! Impossible! I didn't receive Sarah's advice at first. Her pronouncement hit too close to home, sparking some kind of rage in me: *Do you know how hard it is NOT to be hurt right now? Do you know how tough Michael can be sometimes?* However, Sarah lived out her own advice every day, and I witnessed her do it, and I was mature enough to recognize she is one of the most extraordinary women on the planet. So I gave her the benefit of the doubt and resolved to listen to her and think about it, even though I was irked she made it sound so easy.

That night I stayed in a hotel room to really, *really* show Michael how serious I was. (I even chose a pricier hotel to try to piss him off even more.) Our 10-year-old daughter came with me, and our 13-yr-old son stayed home with Michael. I tried to hide my crying while I took a bath, but my wise little princess came into the bathroom, sat on the edge of the tub and told me, "I am here for you, mom. God is in control and he is using this to teach you and dad something. When you learn the lesson, everything is going to be ok." Wow, I should've been *amazed* at that statement coming from my little girl, but instead I got pissed off at TWO more amazing people, first Sarah and now my own daughter. It was getting worse, not better. *Oh Lord, help me.*

It irritated me how they were both simplifying a situation that I was bent on keeping complex: *Michael has no idea of the depths of my suffering from the harsh words he said to me so I have to demonstrate my hurt by staying in this (expensive because I'm mad) hotel room on his credit card while he sleeps alone at home in our lonely bed so he GETS IT and never does it again and then I'm gonna stay hurt to make him pay for the pain he's causing because it's only fair.*

I tried shifting my perspective (something that I had become quite good at) but that wasn't working, either. I just wasn't getting the lesson. I didn't call him that night. Then the next morning I was crushed that he hadn't called me, which is unlike him, *so now I had to make him pay even more.* When he finally did start calling around 10 in the morning *I ignored it.* He texted, "Honey, come home. I love you."

But *clearly he didn't get what he did wrong because his text didn't acknowledge it,* so I turned my phone off. Making him pay was making me *feel* in control but it didn't take the pain away. I dropped Brooke off at home because her grandmother was coming, and I saw that Michael was waiting outside, so I quickly dropped Brooke off on the corner down the street instead. As he started to walk towards the car to catch me, I ignored him and drove calmly away, in hopes he was starting to get the picture. I was acting more ridiculous by the second.

Even my son Jake called me and said, "Mom, if you're trying to make dad pay, just stop. He hasn't moved from the couch in like 12 hours. Please stop punishing him because my sister needs a father and he's a good man."

Ouch. That woke me up. Our children are very respectful, they have grown up in the 'life training' environment and they both know how to share their thoughts in an honorable way, so Jake's request snapped me right out of it. My husband *is* a good man so how could I be *happy* he was hurting? How could my *plan* be *to make him hurt?* I finally went home, and Michael and I talked.

The next day at work I was still a little sore, and we started to go at it again in my office. *I needed him to hear my hurt, so we wouldn't fight on the issue this way again.* While I was talking, Michael was gazing out the window, looking across at the mall.

"Are you listening to me babe? Do you hear how much this hurt me?"

Oh God, I was getting tired of hearing my own pathetic voice. Why couldn't I let go of it?

"It doesn't even feel like you're here with me. Please tell me what you are thinking...*right* this very moment."

He kept staring out the window for a minute and then turned calmly towards me and said, "Honestly? I was just thinking about how much I love it when you can just go over to Macy's and buy yourself something nice."

"What?!" I exclaimed. "What the hell are you talking about?" It felt like we were on two different planets right then.

"You know what really does it for me?" He continued with a smile, gazing out the window as if an entire scene was unfolding in his mind. "When Brooke gets to go shopping at Macy's *with* you. Now *that* really does it for me." (Macy's felt a bit luxurious for us).

From where Michael had come from, the struggles he had had in life, his girls getting to shop at Macy's was a big win at the time. Michael looked so sincerely happy in that moment that it threw me. His smile of joy just disarmed me. It was so random, I just paused and sat back in my chair speechless...and this crazy sort of peace washed over me. *I had wasted four whole days hurting* and I had been pretty committed to staying hurt, but then...it just evaporated in an instant. Why?

As manly as Michael is, in that moment I saw a boy living out *his* dream. After fighting for so many days, he was just exhausted with all the back and forth and had been trying to reach out to me but my unwillingness to let go of the hurt had blinded me and I couldn't see *him* anymore. My heart broke for him. I took a deep breath and smiled away my tears. My *hurt* just didn't matter anymore. Making him pay wasn't getting us anywhere.

Michael simply wanted to make me happy and this sudden boyish daydream he had created in his mind was his version of winning and rescuing his beauty. It didn't really have anything to do with money, even. When he talks about providing, it is never about the *money*. It's about him living out his dream of *us*. It's the picture of making his wife happy that he had imagined since he was a boy.

"Is it really that simple to you?" I asked.

He took a deep breath and smiled, "Yes, it is. Hurting you is the last thing I would ever want to do. I know I am going to make so many mistakes. I'll think more about what you said, but at the end of the day, nothing else matters but seeing you and our children happy and safe."

Our problems seemed to shrink and felt easy to solve in that moment. Simplicity has a way of doing that. His answer revealed what I already knew about men. I was making him pay a price for my complex, emotional need to be heard, understood, appreciated, and acknowledged. A good man *does* appreciate and understand you to the degree a good man can, as Michael had done probably four days earlier, but I had been making it more than it needed to be.

I remembered Sarah reminding me of the price *I* pay when I live in hurt. It robs us. It requires us to build a case against the person we love that damages the relationship. Lingering hurt is a thief that steals our ability to forgive and move forward. Instead, one slight pivot, one shift of our perspective, one quick *decision* can open up a world of possibilities. That day was pivotal in our marriage. Thanks to my choosing to lean on my sisters, Sarah was able to help me with that. It really comes down to *simply deciding ...and then the feelings follow*. When 'hurt' tries to cling to me, I *decide* to let it go. I learned my lesson that day, and we have never had a fight the same, since.

A Good Woman Knows Her Man

It's a bit embarrassing when you can't order for your husband at a restaurant but your best friend can. When this happened more than once, I got a lump in my throat, knowing how well Michael knew *me*. I *thought* I knew everything about him.

It's interesting the stories we tell ourselves to make us feel good. *Of course, I knew my husband! I'm a good wife, I know what makes him happy. I clean up after him, I care for our children, I even mow the lawn, so he doesn't have to sometimes.* But...wait...do I *know* him?

I remember when I heard a training once about the *art of knowing*. Listening to the speaker about knowing your spouse, I kind of got sick to my stomach. I thought his favorite color was blue. Or is it? Or do I just *think* it is because he looks good in it? Then a bunch of scenes started running through my head as I started to think back and look for evidence of how much I really knew Michael. What's his favorite meal? What kind of music does he prefer? What dreams does he have?!? *I am a talker and he's not so it's his fault if he doesn't tell me, right?* Yikes. Hold on.

Let's see, most of the time when I am talking it's about my needs and wants or what the children need or what's coming up next or how we can run the company better or….*Oh, God. I haven't been listening at all.* I felt nauseous. How could this have happened? My prince charming arrived, he rescued me, and he fit the dream but...*I don't know him.* What wife wants to admit that? Maybe you're a good wife who knows everything about him because it's your gifting and it comes easy to you. Or maybe you just *think* you do. But over the years, I have noticed women grow so adamant about being heard that many of us have forgotten how to listen.

Generous listening is powered by curiosity, a virtue we can invite and nurture in ourselves to render it instinctively. - Krista Tippett

God gave us one mouth and two ears respectively, and frankly, when I realized how often I use my mouth and not my ears, I flush with embarrassment. I finally looked at Michael one day and sincerely apologized for not knowing him better, and for my hypocrisy in insisting that he know me so well. And worse, for persecuting him if he didn't remember every detail about me. *Ugh, was I really that self-absorbed?*

Maybe you are super awesome at knowing his likes. Some women are. We may know what his favorite foods are or his hobbies or even something about his work, but do we make it our business to inquire any further beyond that?

You can make it a point to learn what *excites* him. Have you asked him what he loves to do, and then do it with him? Maybe he wants you there, maybe not, but cheer him on either way. Have you asked him about what 'battle' he wants to fight and then encourage him to fight it or train with him to get ready for it? Have you asked him about what kind of adventure he wants to take and let him take it, even if you don't want to join in? Adventure comes in many forms and sometimes you must pay extra attention to notice what it is when it pops up.

A good woman is a student of her man, not the professor. If you are going to really get to know him, then you are going to have to study him. Not once but always, ongoing, forever. To study him does not mean to interrogate him or become a private investigator. The art of knowing a man is to study him without him knowing it. To be curious about who he is, what matters to him, to be an expert at how he communicates, and to understand how he relates to others and to the world. When we are a student for the sole purpose of knowing him, it leads to a deeper connection, an intimacy beyond the physical that will stand the test of time. This kind of pursuit appreciates who he is today and who he wants to be tomorrow. It creates a stronger bond between you, too, as you champion each of his successes, loving him every step of the way. It's what we want our men to do for us, right?

If you are looking for a good man, and you're clear minded about the qualities you are looking for, then you must be a student of him from day one. It never ends and it's a great adventure. If you are still trying to find a good man, you won't have the skill set to identify him if you are not yet prepared and have not first mastered areas of your own life. That's just the way it is. Let's not fall in love with the first guy that gives us attention and miss out on getting to know him in a way that reveals the truth of his character. Be brave, set a guard over your emotions and *study* him first.

As a wife, we often miss out on the excitement of being a continuing student because 'familiarity breeds contempt' over time. We become so familiar with our husbands that we can forget all the reasons we fell in love in the first place. On our wedding day, we have this long list of all the things we love about him. Then, as life happens, we forget the long list and instead pull out a revised list of his shortcomings and start relating to him by that list.

Stop, pull out the list you used on your wedding day (or re-write it)! Remind yourself of the good man you believed him to be and build on that. Burn the list of his inadequacies, since it won't really serve either of you. If you are not yet married, find a good man that you can create a long (realistic) list of his good qualities and character traits, and keep that list out because you will need it when life tries to tear you apart. Rediscover the joy of meditating on the many reasons you are thankful for him by keeping that list in full view and in your heart.

A good woman is a good student of her man, joyfully continuing to discover what he loves and who he wants to be.

A Good Woman Rediscovers

People change. So, what? It is never a reason to break your vows. Irreconcilable differences are a joke in my book. What if you were the one who changed? Would it give him a right to divorce you? He didn't change, you did. Or vice versa. Who cares, really? *Someone* changed because we are in a constant state of change, and often for the better as we get older and wiser. So why are we upset about it? If we are changing, there is a good possibility that it's because we are growing, and that's awesome. So, where's the problem?

Let's take it a step further. When two people divorce, we often hear, "We grew apart. I just don't know him anymore." Well, did you *care* to know?

Maybe we stopped being curious. Maybe we became the professor when we needed to stay the student. Trust me, if you study him and know him, he will notice. If you pull out that long list of your guy's 'pro's' and gratefully act accordingly, he *will* respond because all he wants is a battle to fight, a beauty to rescue and an adventure to live. *You* are not the battle he needs to fight, you need to stay the beauty he wants to rescue and let him live (or join in) his damn adventure!

Today's psychologists and/or media try to convince us this description of a man's role puts unnecessary pressure on men, that it's *not* up to man to rescue you or fight a battle. Why? Because we make this level of responsibility out to be *hard*, instead of celebrating it. Good men want to be this man. It's not their job to make us happy, we must be fulfilled before we marry a good man. I am only suggesting that a good man desires to feel wanted and needed by a good woman and they feel a purpose when they are fighting for good and living an adventure. It is what drives them to succeed.

When we first met I had no idea how important adventure was to Michael. We were working so hard just to learn how to be a couple, and change our lives, and then we were working even harder to build our business, the nonprofit and help change other's lives, that it never occurred to me that he wanted *more*. Then one day after a few thought-provoking comments from my sisterhood, I stepped back and decided to take a deeper look. Michael had changed in so many ways from the contractor guy I had first met. Nowadays, his passions and dreams were coming to life and I could see the joy in his eyes. But I still had to care enough to rediscover all the new ways we related to each other and how I could present myself attractively in a way that made him want to rediscover me, as well. Since I'm the relationship manager, it's my job to lead this discovery.

Michael had always dreamed of being a pilot, I kind of knew that. He didn't talk about it much though, and I was so focused on my dreams and not so much on his. Most women are focused on their own needs until they become mothers and then it's the mom's and the kid's needs…while his gets put on the back burner. We all know how sacrificial women are but honestly, we are often getting our emotional needs met more than his. We should make the decision to intentionally align with his vision, then with discipline and practice, try to stay alongside him in it. We also ought to be careful not to push our man in a direction we 'think' he should go without really inquiring what *he* is dreaming about. And let's not get irritated when our man wants to go live an adventure that doesn't directly involve us or keeps him from home for a bit.

Michael loves to backpack in the Trinity Alps, about 5 hours north of us. I didn't want to participate early on in our marriage, but now I do. He loves his boat, I do, too…*sometimes*. He (subconsciously) measures his success by the size of his toys and so I don't say a word about what he does. He works hard, saves money and puts my wants and the kids' needs before his own. Michael needs to live his adventure. I *know* this about him now because I studied him. I know that he loves to teach others how to push past their fears and if he isn't teaching someone something, he starts to lose his edge, and man, Michael cannot lose his edge. It's his way of keeping score and I want him to win at everything he does. I *know him* now. I don't have to like everything he likes and it's not my job to change his preferences anyway. He loves to win so I help him win.

One day, Michael was missing from work and not answering his phone. It was unusual and the third time within a few weeks. I trust my husband, so I wasn't concerned, but *something* was up and it's usually some crazy new adventure.

I asked one of my best friends if she knew where he was, and she said, "Don't worry. He's doing a great thing."

Her response blew the surprise and she knew it (everyone knows Michaels loves to surprise me). I pressed her for more. "Ok, *what* is he up to?"

"Nothing. What makes you think that?" she nervously responded, avoiding eye contact.

"Um, *duh*. I know my husband." By now, I sure did.

Just then, Michael finally called me back. "Hi *babe*," I greeted him pointedly, "Spill the beans—*what are you up to?*"

He laughed hard. "Hey, I got away with it longer than I thought."

Michael had been studying to get his pilot's license. He had been saving for a year and then secretly taking flying lessons for two months before I found out. He told me he wrote in his journal one day that he dreamed of becoming a pilot, and he had this scenario all planned out in his mind where I was all dressed up and he surprises me by pulling into the airport and leading me to the plane, and then, with amazed tears in my eyes, he flies me over San Francisco Bay into Monterey for dinner. Oh boy. What a vision! Sounded wonderful to me. Michael eventually passed his test, became a pilot and he took me on that date, not so long ago.

I sometimes wonder what either of our lives would look like today if he hadn't come alongside my dream or if I had tried to stop him from living his adventure. At the end of the day, I understand him now and I appreciate his adventures, even if they take him far away from home sometimes.

A good woman makes it her business to know him and when he changes, rediscovers who he has become. She cares about who her good man is *today,* so she can build him up for tomorrow.

A Good Woman Knows Sign Language

If a man talks 25% as much as a woman, how do we get to know him? If a good man goes silent and withdraws when we push him, then how in the world can we know what he wants? If we process verbally and a man processes internally, can we really get to know him? Absolutely.

As I began to study Michael and watch how the other men in my life communicated and how the women in my life complained about men, I made a connection: *men use 'sign language'.* Think about the communication we want from our men. We want them to tell us how they feel about us, tell us "I love you," tell us that they desire us, and that we are beautiful...*because that's how women communicate.* But if actions (signs) speak louder than words, are we missing out on a lot of his communication? If we listen with our eyes, and pay attention to his actions a bit more, study how he communicates with what he *does,* in certain ways it will help us 'hear' what he's been 'saying' all along. Let's not nag, whine, cry and complain that he's not talking to us *the same way that women do verbally,* because *that's not how men naturally communicate.* He *is* communicating, we're just missing it. It's all in sign language. *Watch* and listen.

Michael doesn't give me a ton of compliments. He isn't all over me physically, either, and I used to complain about both non-stop. He really doesn't like to be touched by anyone, but he dishes out a lot of hugs every day of his life because he understands that the hurting women in his life need them. He had to work at it, and still today if he didn't have to hug anyone every again he really wouldn't be bent out of shape about it. For most of our marriage I was hurt by his lack of compliments and all the times I had to tell him I was craving his touch. I'm not into him being all over me, though, so I was a bit of a hypocrite about this for some reason. We were a lot alike in this area, so I was begging him to do something I really didn't do myself. But we do that as women, don't we? I wanted to be touched but not to the degree I was making him pay for. The problem was occasionally I equated his lack of interest with rejection…and that genuinely hurt. I'd start to get clingy and whiny more. I'd convince myself that he was losing interest and act more desperate, which only made him push me away more. (Side note: this is one way to push a man into the arms of another woman.)

Michael would eventually respond when I made a big enough deal over it, because he loved me, and he often said, "The very last thing I ever want you to feel is rejected. I know how horrible that feels."

This cycle continued for years without any results or lasting change. I would complain he didn't touch me enough or compliment me, I'd have a little meltdown over it, he would apologize and for a week he was good about touching me and then, yup, back to the same old pattern. *What the hell?* This was really the worst part of our marriage, the pattern we had the hardest time breaking.

Then one day I had to speak at a meeting, and there was a moment of conflict during the meeting with some of the businessmen. I'm a bit of a straightforward b*tch at times, and Michael knew I had been working hard at being slow to speak and to do so calmly, out of love, so the moment this conflict arose, I took a deep silent breath and instinctually searched the room back and forth for Michael, needing to meet his eyes. I was starting to panic inside, and no one but Michael knew it or could help. Within seconds I met his steady gaze, as he had been waiting for me. He gave the slightest smile and just barely tipped his head at me. No one saw it, it only lasted a moment, but it spoke volumes: *Go ahead, baby. You're ok. You're doing good. Slow down and tell them. Be YOU. Go for it, I've got your back.* His eyes spoke to me.

Guess what? I lit that room on fire! Not only did I make my point, I made an *impact* and changed a lot of minds that day. As I drove home by myself after the meeting, feeling so alive, pondering what had just happened, I got the most precious gift: a flood of memories, times when I was on stage speaking, or at a meeting with the city, or a class I was teaching, or a talk show I was invited on…and there was Michael, always in the back, always waiting for my eyes to meet his if I needed them.

I began to cry. *Hard.* My heart filled with gratitude and sorrow for having missed it all this time. Michael had been 'speaking' to me his love and strength and support this whole time in his 'sign language'…and I *missed* it. As many times as I complained, he never once reminded me how many times and ways he *was* communicating to me. The memories were countless! I realized how often and even in the smallest of circumstances, when the slightest of fears tried to consume me, my eyes searched for his and he was there, every time…steady, encouraging, cheering me on, coaching me into victory, WITHOUT A SINGLE WORD SPOKEN.

I rushed home to him that night, crying tears of gratitude and asking forgiveness for never seeing it before. I shared with him how God had blessed me with that sudden flood of memories. Do you know what he did? He gave me the sweetest hug, holding me close, like I always asked him to. He looked down at me, smiling, as if he knew this day was coming, and said, "Honey, it's what I love to do best."

I spent so many years thinking I was not getting my needs met when it came to intimacy. Then I read this:

Intimacy means *in-to-me-see.*

Oh my Lord, I'd been so wrong! Michael was most certainly seeing and being in-to-me.

For a solid week I mulled this over. I'd be driving and some new memory would come to mind, some situation where Michael showed up in a way that I didn't expect him to: when he worked endless hours so we could go on a vacation, or when I'd hear him and Brookie in the other room giggling, or when he was teaching

Jake, our son, how to respect me. There were many times he got up in the middle of the night to take a call from a woman trying to escape an abusive man or talk to a drunk man that just needed to hear the voice of hope. I was reminded of the nights he spent painting one of our stores a new color just because I changed my mind or how he went to my father for my hand in marriage (I had no idea he'd done that). He sat quietly in the shadows as I received so much recognition for the success of Crossing the Jordan. I would be given an award and he was the first to congratulate me, never saying a word about how much effort he had put into it. I realized if it weren't for him and God's grace, none of it would have been possible.

Men speak in sign language. A good man speaks in sign language. Sisters, we just aren't paying attention. Either we are trying to force them to verbalize emotionally more, like women, or we are taking their silence as rejection. The greatest way a woman can discover how a good man communicates is to watch and then encourage the *good*. Encourage and honor him with your own words. Acknowledge the good that you see and quietly pray for the bad to get better. Men love to hear the good and guess what, he'll start doing better if you continue focusing on believing the best in him.

A good man signs, telling you what kind of man he really is. Are you watching? Are you listening?

A Good Woman Trusts

Hang on to your seat, girl. This one's the toughest of them all.

Once you are a woman prepared to be in a committed relationship and have found your good man or are currently married, you must trust him...NO MATTER WHAT!

I can hear the responses already, *He's not trustworthy! He's sneaky, he cheated already so there's no way I can trust him.* Here's one that's used a lot: *Trust is earned. I won't trust him until he has earned it.* Sorry, sister, you must *trust* this man, no matter what he has done and no matter how he is acting. Yes. I said, under *all* circumstances. (The only exception is physical, continual abuse.) That includes cheating. (Oh boy, am I going to get crap for this one).

Here we go: *You must accept a good man exactly as he is, and in no way, and I mean absolutely never, control him or try to change him.* This means that good man (or the man you are married to) can NEVER receive correction of any kind from you...ever...for any reason. At least not in the way women typically correct their husbands.

Hold on. I'll explain. Let's break it down: if he cheated on you and you are still married to him, *you made the choice already to stay.* The only problem now is your intention to make him 'pay' for what he has done, going forward. This is where we go wrong. This applies to all issues, not just cheating. *Not* trusting him will *not* get you the results you want. You must trust him *nooooooo maaaaaattttterrrrrr whaaaaat.* Get it? Trust is like an insurance policy for the marriage: just because he has placed a claim every so often doesn't mean you can cancel the policy! You must immediately cover him the second he turns in his claim. Remember the whole 'for better or for worse' vow?

Back when I was dating my husband, he worked construction and had a great body (he still does) and easily attracted women because of his masculinity. One day he looks at me and says,

"You never question me. Not ever. You never check on me and you are never suspicious. Why?"

I said, "Because I trust you."

You see, I had already learned this lesson before I met Michael. Checking his phone, his whereabouts or becoming the private investigator in the relationship never stops a man from cheating, ever. Period. NEVER. So if it won't stop him, why do it? Guess what he might do if you keep not trusting him? Cheat. Why? Because a mistress *wouldn't* be nagging, pressuring, and acting all crazy suspicious with him. She would be telling him everything *he* wants to hear. (At least at first.)

Have you ever been cheated on and find out later that the women he cheated with isn't as pretty or successful as you are? (I don't care how that sounds because we all think it.) I have, and I've heard this uncomfortable observation from a lot of women. It's not something we like to admit out loud but, ultimately, we're like...*What the hell? Why HER?* I don't want to put down other women based on appearances or anything, so calm down, it's just some women aren't living out their full potential, at every season of their lives. Half the time, the mistresses are unaware at first that they are even the mistress! This is about how a man wants a woman that encourages him, lifts him up and makes him feel like superman. That's the main reason why men cheat. Most of the time it's not about the sex, *it's about the approbation they are getting.* The definition of approbation: approval, acceptance, endorsement, appreciation, respect, admiration, esteem, commendation, praise...*all the things a man is desiring from a woman!* (Remember that word, approbation, it's a good one!)

That all said, it's about the trust that we extend them and how a man relates to that trust. Remember I mentioned how men trust differently than women. Our lack of trust manifests into always checking in on them, nagging at them to come home, giving off an uneasy vibe or just coming off straight up insecure, all of which makes us unattractive. I want you to be free of these desperate behaviors and instead rock his world with all that you have to offer. Let's lead with who we *are* and not from who we are afraid we *could* be (the victim).

When my husband and I were still dating, he liked to drink. A LOT. One night, he got drunk and cheated on me. (Most people don't know this because we have this fairytale happily-ever-after type of marriage, but life happens, then you must build what you want.)

He had one too many after work one day on the job site and found himself in a very stupid situation. He never was one to stay out late so I did have a sick feeling that evening. We weren't married yet, but we were in a committed relationship. I chose to let that icky feeling pass and just trust him.

A friend of his called me some time later and told me what happened, and Michael confessed immediately. This was one of the hardest moments of my life because I knew I had to practice what I preach. I had trusted him unconditionally...*and still got hurt.* Maybe this level of sacrifice seems like weakness to you. I would have thought the same, before. But now I knew what an immature emotional response would get me, and I had matured, been praying for Michael, and watching him grow. He was a good man that occasionally struggled to soar. He had the characters and qualities I had longed to see in a man. My own father saw Michael as a good man, so I also had feedback from loved ones that he was a man of innate good character. But at this point in his life, he certainly should not have been drinking.

So, I had a choice to make: would I continue to trust him no matter what? Or would I not forgive, and just walk away? I also knew that if I did decide to trust, I would have to forgive him and not withdraw my trust insurance policy.

I chose, wisely, to stay. Michael was more remorseful than I had ever witnessed a man to be. He asked for my forgiveness and I extended it. I was an experienced, prepared-for-commitment woman and I knew how to forgive. He was a *good* man, who made a terrible impulsive mistake, and you know what? It happens. It hurt me, but that moment of choice I made to forgive was also an extraordinary spiritual experience...I was filled with peace and a calm sense of certainty. That forgiveness was the most precious gift I have ever given. It impacted our children and countless others we serve today.

To this day, I have never used that mistake as a weapon against Michael, only to share with others the power and freedom forgiveness has. The best part is that it didn't end up being a struggle for me because, through forgiveness, no bitterness ever took root in me. Additionally, through the gift of my unconditional trust, my husband changed that day. *Michael knew in that moment that I was the one he had been waiting his entire life for.* The very day I said, "I forgive you" was the very day my husband poured his last drink. Michael has never drunk a drop of alcohol nor smoked anything since that moment over 10 years ago now.

The love of a good woman is powerful, and the love of an honorable man can lead his family into all they were destined to be.

One act of forgiveness can set your life on a course you never imagined was possible.

A good woman knows what she is called to do and does it, with elegance and kindness, not keeping record of his wrongs or demanding payment for the hurt. A good woman can architect any life that she desires. *Be* a good woman.

Chapter 7

Sisterhood

I didn't used to *like* women. It's the story I told myself for as long as I can remember. I mean, I *tried* to like other women…I *guess*. Most of the time, my dislike was on a subconscious level and only on occasion, when I had gotten *really* hurt, would I consciously think *I don't like women*. I fed that story whenever I felt rejected or betrayed by another woman. Jealousy was never an issue with me, however, because I've just personally never struggled with that (which honestly is just a straight-up God-given gift because of how He intended to use me in the future). I also didn't *hate* women or feel necessarily at odds with them all the time, I just didn't like them enough to hold any value with or put any effort into creating relationships with them.

I told myself that men were safer to hang out with: less dramatic, never jealous, more easygoing, and didn't backbite. After telling myself this story for so long I became more and more isolated, which awoke in me a growing longing for a sisterhood that I just couldn't ignore. I knew there was something missing from my life with regard to women, but I filled that hole with men and the instant gratification of their physical affections. I felt empty, though, and increasingly alone in a way that the endorphin rush of his attentions became like a drug, and like a drug, I found myself needing more and more to feel the effects.

My bad choices in men also seemed to repel good women, and I didn't know how to fix that, much less ask for help. I wanted bad men, even if they weren't good for me. The shame I felt over that just further reminded me I wasn't as good as other women…which further distanced me from people…where the only person able to reach me on my lonely island was the bad man I had chosen to be with at the time.

I remember playing with girl friends in grade school, how the hell did I end up in my 20's as an isolated, empty soul with no female friends? The truth was I didn't even know *how* I had gotten to the place where I stopped trusting women altogether. My 'dislike' towards women was really just a cover for that bewilderment, a mask to hide my loneliness behind. I longed for connection but I didn't know how to articulate it, even though it was there, right beneath the surface. I cried myself to sleep often, hoping and praying someone would hear my silent cry for help.

Since I couldn't seem to stop the cycle of dating abusive men (as if I were a walking neon sign saying 'treat me badly') I became anxious out in public, believing other women would spot me for the mess I was and judge me. I was shriveling into a kind of depression I didn't understand. My weak attempts at reaching out only brought more pain when no woman wanted to deal with my unhealthy behaviors.

I eventually became suicidal. It seemed as if I couldn't take one more breath alone, lost and scared. My thoughts tortured me: *I want to die. Wait, my daughter...Chelsea...my sweet angel. How would she ever forgive me? How could I abandon her? How selfish would it be to take my own life?* The more alone I felt, in the throes of an abusive relationship, the more intense the thoughts became. Then finally I heard: *Chelsea will be better off without you. Just end it all.*

Thankfully, those thoughts cut off suddenly the day I was arrested, and I found myself surrounded by thousands of women I had told myself I didn't like or trust. This was one of the single most significant moments of my life. Women, everywhere: young, old, some very lost and very not nice, but many brave and strong women that had learned from their mistakes and were ready to comfort me and guide me through my pain. I finally began to see women in a new way. I couldn't believe it took me wanting to end my life to find the beginning of it, where it should have always been—in a village of women relying on each other to get through life *well* together.

So, I had a choice: would I choose to love? Or would I stay in my 'prison' of loneliness, a far darker place than the current one surrounding me with barbed wire fences. I could sense freedom waiting for me...so I chose to love.

What Happened to Us?

If you were to ask the majority of women (especially those that are currently hurting) why they don't reach out to their 'sisters,' you would be saddened by their response. They don't see other women as a genuinely viable resource to help them solve their problems. We are so disconnected in today's culture and unaware of how it's affecting our everyday lives and our *souls*.

I was born in the early 70's. (You young woman keep on reading, I'm still relevant!) I believe my generation of women was the last to experience true intimate connection with each other, but by our mid 20's it was already beginning to fade. Our apartment doors used to face toward courtyards where we gathered and got to know one another. Front yards were used more than backyards. Kids played with other neighborhood kids and there was a bond between neighbors. Then as our world expanded with more information, we started to shrink inside, keeping our children under lock and key because the world was getting more dangerous. It's ironic because I believe *that lack of connection* is one cause of the danger, it's at the source of our mental health issues and crime. I am not sure which came first, the chicken or the egg, but the result is we have become *isolated people.*

Imagine this scenario in the 1950's. A woman gets in a fight with her husband. Upset, she crosses the street in her hair curlers to her neighbor, who at one glance at her friend's face immediately puts the coffee on, sits down and slaps an ashtray and a pack of cigarettes on the table as if she has set this scene many times before. The wife cries and the neighbor listens. Divorce wasn't the go-to answer for solving marital problems like it is today. Irreconcilable differences weren't enough (even legally) to give up on your marriage or your family. People *stayed* committed. So, women leaned on each other. They listened to the council of the women that went before them. Their marriages weren't perfect, either, but there was long-refined wisdom to tap into, and those 'sisters' worked it out together. They didn't process with other men, they processed with other women and heavily relied on each other.

My mother was born in a tiny cabin in Alabama, and when her family moved west she met my father. They then settled in Northern California, which was quite a different culture from where she'd been raised. Supper was a thing in my house, and coffee and girl talk was also very important in the order of things. My parents managed apartment complexes while I was growing up and because of my mother's southern hospitality, she always created a village wherever we lived. Snacks at the pool with the tenants and coffee on her porch with the neighbors was a common part of our lives. I remember that community started to fade as I got into my late teens. People stopped participating in the 'village' activities as much. When families moved out, the new neighbors just stayed inside. I saw it begin to take toll on my mother: she grew quiet and anxious from the loss of intimacy, the longing for knowing what was going on with her neighbors, the lack of connection. My mother was a passionate woman and not the best communicator, so she would sometimes force involvement with her neighbors, to her own detriment at times, as her world began to shrink and become more isolated.

I was a strong-willed and rebellious teenager during this time because my parents did not present a united front of agreement and that allowed me to divide them…they were young and doing their best. I remember thinking they were raising me in a way that conflicted with the way the world was heading, so I began to see my mother's wisdom as 'control' and her guidance as being 'out of touch' with reality. Boy, was I wrong. My mother's gone now, she passed when she was only 53, but what I wouldn't give to tell her how *right* she was about pretty much everything. Her communication methods absolutely sucked, really, but I remember knowing deep down that her wisdom rang true, even then. The culture was shifting, I was getting sucked into it and had no idea of the consequences of my self-rule. Independence? Um, no, more like utter foolishness for not acknowledging the experience of the women before me.

R-E-S-P-E-C-T

Have you ever thought *why can't it be between women how it used to be?* As I was writing this section of the book, I literally asked a bunch of young women (including those not in my tribe) this question. I asked if they wished they had more girlfriends. *Every single one said yes, and confessed how alone they felt, even among their existing group of friends.* I asked them if they wished that they had listened to the warnings of older or wiser women about a certain man or situation. I got a resounding, "Hell, *yeah*, I wish I had listened!"

I do recognize that many of these lessons are unavoidable. We'll all feel heartache over a guy someday, we'll all make mistakes growing up, and that's been going on since the beginning of time. I appreciate how pain can be tool for learning, but it's better to avoid unnecessary pain by heeding others' wisdom. Humans are designed to be in community, and one of the purposes of community is to learn from one another. The generations before us were doing *something* right: in 1901 there was an 8% divorce rate, in 1950 a 26% divorce rate. Compare that to today's 50%. Going forward, the sanctity of marriage may cease to exist. We *want* to be married. We love the beauty and the security of being committed 'until death do us part'. We innately comprehend the benefits of having someone committed to you, no matter what, till the end.

There is a very loud MINORITY that seeks to remove marriage altogether, but the majority of us (if we stay vigilant about what's happening) will prevail because monogamy is wired into our DNA and God created marriage for our benefit, as a species. I obviously don't care about being politically correct, here, I just don't want hurting women to stay trapped in their belief system. If women dig deep and get honest, we are reminded of the truth of what we collectively know we desire as women: a faithful good man to marry. Since this is true, why not lean on the women in our lives that have learned to *stay* married?

If you've divorced, I get it. Michael is my second marriage, too. I was not ready or equipped to be a married woman in my first marriage and had no skill how to make the marriage work. I picked a husband for all the wrong reasons and I did not listen to the women in my life that warned me to not even date him. I never wanted to end the marriage but drugs ruled my ex-husband and so we divorced, despite my efforts to stay married. Michael had the identical scenario in his previous marriage.

We've lost the respect for the wisdom of our elders, or for other women, for that matter. I believe it is because we do not want the accountability required of us when asking for help. We are increasingly diminishing an extremely valuable resource: our older 'sisters' and that authentic, get-all-up-in-your-business-kind of sisterhood. Since the older generations were 'oppressed' or 'too conservative' or whatever-the-hell we've made up, in our way of thinking it discounts the extremely valuable wisdom of their experiences, so we 'throw out the baby with the bathwater' and go at it alone, bereft of their guidance. Not only is that foolish, it's dishonorable.

Signs of Hope

I do see a shift in our culture with all this talk of 'finding your tribe', though. The #bossbabe movement and other similar groups have created a new awareness of the need to connect, and I love that. Unfortunately, many of the groups' feminist mindsets taint the messages with ideas that dishonor men. Church groups can sure improve, as well, since they are often shallow, only meet once a week, don't connect on a deeper level outside of the group or aren't willing to do *whatever it takes* to support the hurting souls…within their members *or* outside the church walls. Helping people can get messy, it's uncomfortable, and if it can't fit it into our busy schedules, we don't want to bother.

Thankfully there are many successful sisterhoods among us, but for the everyday girl, they are hard to find and even harder to break in to. The bigger issue is that since we are so far down the disconnection road that, even if there are groups available, women feel so isolated and unworthy that they lack the courage to join. Sometimes they are adult children, unlikable and messy, and other women just don't want to deal with them.

We need to get over it! That's what humanity is all about, connecting! Yeah, it's messy and emotional and draining at times… *and* the most precious, rewarding part of life! Try being selfish for an extended period of time and then tell me how your life looks. Why not get authentic and real with another woman, help her out of her suffering, and guide her to live her best life? Now *that* is worth its weight in gold no matter who you are. When we serve others or give selflessly, everything else has the potential to miraculously fall into place, not because our circumstances have changed but because our perspective has. Let's begin to respect those that have gone before us again and appreciate the cost of their contribution to our lives. Let's build a sisterhood of mighty women that can bind together, live generously and amazingly with one another.

Look In the Mirror

I remember the first day I *looked* at myself in the mirror. I don't mean look at my face or my hair or check to see if I needed some lipstick. I mean, when *I really looked at myself.* It was a dark day for me. I had just sobered up after pretty much destroying my life and crushing my little girls' heart. I was so lost that I just had this crazy desire to look into my own eyes, me, Dana, and ask myself *who I was and why I had done this.* It was a first step towards bravery. I couldn't run from, avoid, drown out, numb or kill the woman I had become so I had *better* get to know her. I looked in the mirror and said, "Hi, I'm Dana," out loud. I stood there staring for a while. It's a weird experience, especially when I had spent so many years trying to avoid really seeing the woman that I had become. "Hi, I'm Dana," I said to myself again. "Nice to meet you," I smiled and answered. "We have a lot of work to do." And I kind of chuckled out loud. It was a tender, simple sort of moment. I needed simple. I'd been running so long and so hard and the mess I had created was so big, I had to take a deep breath and start…somewhere…somehow.

My journey really began that day. God showed up for me in my brokenness. In prison I had to make the best of my circumstance, discover who I really was and be willing to grow up. I had come to the realization that my quest to 'do it alone or 'do it my way' wasn't working. The lies were done. I could look in my own eyes and state the truth: that I've *not* been a good person to others and that my attitudes, dishonesty, and selfishness were the reason I was here. I could finally *own up* to my shit.

God gently and lovingly opened my eyes to who I had become, bringing to mind the times I had hurt other women while complaining that they had hurt me. Times I had been longing to be rescued by someone but wasn't looking to help anyone else at all. As I gazed at myself in the mirror, I asked myself, was I even likable? Was I kind or did my problems come first? Did I ever listen or was I too busy talking? Was I a giver or a taker? I wasn't a good friend and frankly, with all the love I *thought* I had in my heart to give, I still had become shallow, cold and self-serving… and it was no longer a mystery why I didn't have a sisterhood. *I* wasn't a good sister.

I met myself that day. I wasn't miraculously fixed of all my bad behaviors and I still had quite a road ahead of me, but I do know light flooded in, through my willingness to look at myself in the mirror, and through the grace of God, my surrender to who I was chased away the darkness. I looked at myself one last time and promised, "I will *become* a good sister and I will *be* a good friend and mother."

Cleaning Up the Hood

By the time I met Michael, I had been out of prison for over 5 years but still had not connected with other women the way I had in prison. I was embarrassed to admit to myself that I missed prison! I missed that deep connection, openness and vulnerability—and accountability—among trusted sisters. Clearly, I loved my freedom, but I had experienced something so deep and precious there, that to suddenly not have it left a hole in my soul. I longed for that intimacy.

I searched for it. Over time, I went back to some old, sort-of-safe relationships I had in my youth. I gained a handful of new women friends. I had tried to develop a tribe when I first got out from prison but because some of those earlier efforts ended up in rejection I was afraid. So, over time, I found myself making very little effort into finding the kind of women that would love me for me and hold me accountable for going after my dreams. I *settled* for just a few friends. I stopped searching for more.

One day Michael asked about an old friend of mine I had reconnected with. "So, tell me again why she's your friend?"

"What?" I asked, irritated at the question.

"I mean, I don't even get what makes her a *friend* to you," he pressed.

"Michael, we've been friends for 15 years."

"Oh, I know. You have to keep telling me." He answered with a smile.

"I'm a loyal person." I snapped.

"I know what *you* are. Just tell me what about *her* that makes her a

good friend to *you*."

"*She's my best friend!*"

"I know. But *why*?" He continued. "All I see is her taking from you, putting you down to make herself feel better, and never supporting your dreams."

I was speechless.

"Honey, you deserve the support." Michael finished, kissed my head and walked away (his standard way of delivering a sensitive message).

Ouch. It hurt to hear him say that and hurt more to realize it was true. My old friends had me in a box. They wanted the old Dana, the one they felt superior to. I realized many of them always had.

Michael had been supportive of my friends up to that point. He'd hang out with them and invite them over, for my sake, and even though I'd catch his eyes rolling at some of them when they'd leave the room, he never made them feel unwelcome, unless it was to defend me. On a few occasions he openly challenged their insensitive comments towards me and they'd retort, calling him rude, but Michael couldn't help but defend me. It was odd how I hadn't noticed their comments in the past the way I was beginning to hear them now.

It took some time to wrestle through what he said that day. I spent more than a week reflecting on the relationships I had, including some old ones since high school. Because I was loyal by nature, I didn't just *end* relationships, I kept them open. Also I kept them because if I ever felt alone I would have *someone* who cared.

But Michael's words struck me in such a way that I suddenly felt free, and had permission, to *choose*. I took an inventory of my past and current relationships to see if they were even in line with my vision for my life.

I have always had an entrepreneurial spirit and a creative mind. I remember sharing my crazy ideas often with family or friends. One day at dinner, in my early 20's, a family member poked fun at me by saying, "The only way Dana will ever make money is to write a book, *A Hundred Ways How to Make Money*".

"What?" I asked, confused, as the entire family chuckled loudly.

"Your ideas, Dana. You always talk about your *ideas*. The only way you'll be successful is to try to con people into thinking your ideas will work."

My eyes began to well up. I tried to hide it. "You're right." I laughed with them. "Well, at least that book might sell."

I excused myself and ran to the bathroom, crying. When I returned to the table, no one even noticed my red eyes. I realized then it was a habit that everyone was comfortable with, to make fun of Dana's ideas and dreams. I never noticed when that had started, and had no idea how to make it stop.

Over the years, I had somehow allowed these types of people to speak into my life. When Michael said those words, it was like a parade of people's faces going by, in my mind, all of them the same: relating to me as a woman who will never do what she said she was going to do. Somehow, I had acquiesced to all this, giving them permission to make me feel little, and incapable.

That was another life-changing conversation moment with Michael. I could be a giver and serve unselfishly, putting myself out there for others, and *not have to accept or put up with any takers*, sucking me dry with their negativity. I could *choose* who I allowed to speak into my life.

I needed cheerleaders, not doubters. I needed believers and not dream killers. I had chosen to love others, but I had to love myself enough to be more careful of who I kept as my *sisters*. I had to clean up my 'hood' and I had to do it quickly. I took some time to explain to a few of those friends how I reached this decision, and their reactions only proved that I had made the right choice to let them go. The others just faded into the distance when I stopped taking the brunt of their jokes.

It's kind of crazy how I've always been talented and ambitious yet allowed the words of a few to affect me so much, in a way that crushed my dreams. It's easy to say when we are on the other side of the pain, but we let it happen, don't we? Why do we let the words and opinions from people we don't admire or respect, or who don't respect us, affect our future?

Well, sister, *I* am a *good* friend and I am telling you that you are worth more than you know, and you can accomplish your dreams, especially with a tribe of woman that lifts you up and cheers you on towards them (even if they sound crazy!) As you go after your goals, you'll need to figure out the way. You may stumble, you'll likely bump your head, but life has a way of teaching us from those hard lessons, and your sisterhood will carry you when life kicks your ass. They'll hold you through any suffering, allow you to have a 15-minute pity party and then say, "Get up! Just go at it a different way, girl, you've got this!" Those sisters can help walk you through to the life you have been waiting to have.

How to Be a Good Sister

It's time to reflect on our own character as a sister, for a moment. I am counting on your maturity to honestly ask yourself: *Do you think you are a good sister?* (Remember, we are not lying to ourselves anymore. The first step in transformation is to become *aware* of our current reality.)

Do you ask how people's days are, actually caring about the answer, or do you start talking about yours first? Do you know about your friends' likes and dislikes, their children's struggles, their memorable family moments, their birthdays, and their dreams and aspirations? Do you send out thank you cards, or know how they like their coffee?

Are you likable? Do you smile, or do you have a resting bit** face and say that's just the way you are? For years, I got feedback that I looked mean or too busy to interrupt. The complaints were annoying at first. I thought people were just whining or being a wuss, until I realized how arrogant it was to think that way, and they probably just wanted to connect. So, after making excuses for years, I decided *this isn't really how I want people to experience me,* and started smiling when I spoke, and stopped to say hi in passing. I changed my countenance, and altered the experience people were having of me. My face wasn't matching my heart anyway, really, because I love people. I love making them feel good. I cannot tell you the joy it has brought me just to smile more. I am literally a happier person just from that simple, small, intentional act.

Being likeable to other women is something we just don't pay attention to. We walk around like we are entitled to a good man AND a good sisterhood. We wonder why other women don't like us and then we refuse to change the things that make us unlikable.

I also want to ask you this: *Are you a victim?* (This one's a doozy.) I was the biggest victim for years, *and I couldn't stand victims.* What a hypocrite, right? When we are trapped in a victim mindset, we repel even the nicest of people. No one wants to be in an intimate relationship with someone that embodies that hopeless, negative mentality. It's like an extinguisher of joy and draining to be around. It breeds death, not life. As a constant victim, we not only don't attract good sisters, the only people left that will buy into your bullcrap are codependents or other victims competing *with you* to see who the bigger victim is. It's sick and sad and your life cannot flourish stuck down in the muck of this mindset. We need to move from victim to victor. We will get there! Stick with me in these coming chapters, because if you do not kill the 'victim' inside you, it will kill *you.*

Girl, be willing to do what it takes to become a good sister and attract the sisterhood you've always needed and wanted. It starts with sowing in others' lives what we want to have in our own. If you want people to believe in you, start *believing* the best in others. If you don't want people to gossip about you, stop gossiping. If you want trust, then be trustworthy. If you want someone to be kind to you, be a kind person. If you want to receive, be a giver.

Be intentional about EVERYTHING you do, your thoughts, actions, goals, and all your relationships. You are not random matter floating through life, and neither are the people who come across your day. Each moment has, and YOU have, a purpose—and a limited time of one life to accomplish it—so draw up the roadmap to the life you want and the kind of friend you need to be to get the type of sisterhood you crave. Plan it and they will come.

Build Your Tribe

Your vibe attracts your tribe. Have you heard this one yet? It's popular because it rings true. Which comes first, our vibe or our tribe? We need our tribe to strengthen our vibe, but we won't attract a strong tribe if we don't have a solid vibe. I promise you, the benefits of living within a strong, connected community far outweigh any issues you might have with people. Focus on being a good sister and the rest will work out.

Our marriages will be stronger as well, if we have a sisterhood, because a good man wants us to connect with other women. He shouldn't have to process the things with you that you should be processing with other women. When you are surrounded by solid sisters you have intentionally decided to trust NO MATTER WHAT, any bad man will be exposed at warp speed, saving you from misery and wasted time. Basically, *all the world's problems can be solved through sisterhood! (mic drop)*

Really, it's true, though, but it's just not *easy* finding this type of sisterhood. I couldn't. I didn't know where to start. It also finally dawned on me that I didn't like to be vulnerable because I didn't want to risk rejection, again.

I knew I needed to just walk up to a woman, smile and say, "Hey, I would love to take you out to lunch."

I knew I just had to be bold and ask. I had to be likeable, kind, authentic and real, even raw, so I tried...and got my feelings hurt a few times. However, I learned that the better my attitude, the more positive the response. I started serving women in my community, mentoring the brokenhearted and speaking hope into their lives. That connected me with other women that cared and served. Then, my love for people started to be contagious, and I inspired others to help. I started to meet one amazing woman after another. I started to frequent the same activities as them. I also attended transformational trainings, meeting even more extraordinary women, becoming their friends as well.

Then we founded Crossing the Jordan and I became a leader in my community, with even more influence. I just kept giving and serving and serving and giving some more. By then, I was more discerning about what type of women was best to have in my tribe. I'd been around the block, so I could spot a taker or a hater a mile off, and I just avoided those women. (In time they didn't even approach me anymore).

The more you seek, the more you find. You will find women that add incredible value to your life because they are divinely appointed for you to connect, support, and guide you. It's crazy now to see how much of a ripple effect my life has had because I chose to be vulnerable and *become* a good sister. I look around and see all my dreams coming true: I'm leading a tribe of ba-dass women of excellence, who are warriors fighting the good fights, pursuing *their* purpose, and helping other women to pur-sue theirs.

If you cast your vision for sisters, being kind and courageous, you will build your tribe. Maybe no one will knock on your door at first, but you can knock on theirs. God loves connecting us in mysterious ways. Get your good vibe on, girl, your sisters are out there, waiting for you!

Chapter 8

Self-Possession

Self-Possession

When I first heard the word 'self-possessed' I didn't like it much. It sounded negative, selfish even. I felt I had wasted too much time already being 'all about me.' Since my life transformed, I'd been about self-sacrifice. Even the term 'self-help' sounds a bit arrogant and irritating to me because I tried that, and it don't work, girlfriend, not on its own.

I need a God. I need my tribe (sisterhood). So, I'm hypersensitive to any personal growth advice that focuses on relying on self exclusively to do to anything. I'm tough, and not reliant on people in a way that's unhealthy, but I have found great freedom in understanding and accepting our interdependence on one another.

Sarah, my trusted confidant, shared the meaning of the term self-possession with me, so I investigated it.

The Definition of Self-Possession: calm, confident, and in control of one's feelings; composed.

Synonyms: assured, self-assured, calm, cool, composed, at ease, unperturbed, unruffled, confident, self-confident, poised, imperturbable; together, unfazed, nonplussed, unflappable.

I like how that definition made me *feel.* It described who I believe myself to be today. It is how I hear other women describe me. In fact, I have trained myself to embody this type of woman: composed, confident, together, poised, self-assured. Being this type of woman *is* my vision. I have arrived. Well, sort of.

We are all a work in progress. I get frazzled more than I would like to admit, I am not as calm at times as I could be, sometimes I'm straight-up crazy and on many days, girl, I just don't have it together at all. Still, I *knew* who I wanted to become and so I *became.* I made a plan. When my journey began, I only knew who I *didn't* want to be. Then once I decided who I wanted to be, I had to figure out how to get there. Maybe you're already self-possessed, or maybe you *think* you are. Either way, we can always learn and should never stop growing.

I am constantly learning how to be a better human. I read, watch videos, attend trainings, and reach out to those that can teach me. I am almost always in a forward motion. It's an adventurous way to live! I hope you take what you can from this book and let it sink in where it needs to. We can all use a kick in the butt when we are stuck, we can heal up where we may be hurting, and could use some encouragement when we just want to run and hide.

Be Forgiving

This is an obvious one to start with: we can't move forward until we have forgiven others and ourselves. We hear this often, but do we *really* forgive? The best description of forgiveness I've ever heard is to 'take your hands off their throat,' letting go of the *active focus* of anger towards someone. In my experience, most people who find themselves stuck have unforgiveness, and either they aren't aware of it or they just refuse to forgive. What I do know is unforgiveness is the deadliest of poisons.

Unforgiveness turns into bitterness and bitterness takes root. It gets into the innermost parts of your being, then it seeps out in the nastiest ways and it is the number one repellent to not only a good man but a good life, in general. Bitterness is like a dog whistle that only good people can hear. A bitter person can't see it on themselves: the resentful, defensive attitude, like a cloud, hovering over them everywhere they go. It takes an outside perspective to see that bitter cloud. Since misery loves company and like attracts like, bitter people are often attracted to other bitter people, so they can lick their wounds together, and remind each other of how victimized they are. Over time, a bitter person begins to shrivel, the hardness of their heart taking its toll on their soul, their health, even their face. They made themselves a bitter old maid and they don't even see it. It is a sad life, and good men don't want bitter old maids.

I could fill a hundred pages with a hundred stories of how being a victim, and not forgiving, will kill you. I've watched bitter women use drugs to numb the pain until they literally killed themselves. I've witnessed a beautiful, gorgeous woman age quickly and brutally due to the bitter poison running through her veins, and I have seen many bitter women ruin a good marriage over unforgiveness.

I have great respect for how difficult the process is for many to *let go*. However, in mentoring hundreds of women at this point in my life, I have plenty of experience of seeing the results that come from both forgiveness and unforgiveness. One leads to life, the other to death, period. No way around it.

I understand the acts that have been committed against some of you are *horrific*. I have cried my eyes out walking out through this process with women that have gone through gang rapes, molestation by family members, and beatings so bad they barely lived. I personally have been tortured by a man, strangled, had my nose broken, been treated like a dog begging for my life. Oh God, do I understand grief and suffering. The truth is that the size of a person's wrongs against you doesn't matter, because each act requires forgiveness for *you* to be set free.

I will never forget one of the first women I began to walk through this process with. I was in rehab waiting to get sentenced. She was a prostitute on the streets before she came in and had been in a sexual relationship with her *biological* father prior to that. It took some time for me to figure the story out, but it finally came out, that her father had been raping her since she was five. He tortured, brainwashed, and slept with her hundreds of times and later sold her body to others. Nothing is worse than stripping the innocence from a child. And then making it the fault of the child? Oh God, there is just nothing sicker here on this earth. Even worse, she seemed to be fine with it!

My father in an honorable man and I could not even fathom how this could be. I wanted to shout at her and shake her as she made light of it all. I wanted to judge her and run away from the responsibility of helping her and frankly, from my own disgust. Instead, I loved her, and as frustrated as I was, I was willing to walk out the dark stuff. We chose to include her in our community of sisters, we held her as the staff instructed us, to just *be* there with her. But I was young and impatient, and *oh Lord*, was it hard to not just flip out and scream, "This is disgusting!"

I remember very clearly the day that she woke up to the truth. We had gained her trust, and it was time. We women were in a circle around her, when I looked her straight in the eyes and said, "This isn't right, and I believe you know it now and want to be free from him."

She wailed for three straight hours. I held her tightly. We all wept with her, for hours and hours. Time stood still. She screamed, "NO!" at the top of her lungs so loud it shook the walls. She punched the floor and tossed the chairs. We let her. We didn't care. None of us were shaken by her outbursts. We had been waiting for this day, when the denial could no longer hide the pain of the truth, and as a good tribe of women we wouldn't let her be alone in her suffering.

A few times over those hours, she would stop and whimper and grab both of my cheeks and desperately draw my face to hers with terror in her eyes, crying, "How could he do this to me? How could I let this happen?"

"It's not your fault," I just kept whispering, "It's not your fault."

I had faced the evilest of evils. Those days changed me forever, not because of the evil she went through but because of the days, weeks and months that followed: walking through it together, crying together, punching pillows, swearing a whole lot, laughing together and peeing our pants more than once. (When you are exhausted and get the giggles, it just happens). I participated in the transformation of this dead woman walking as she began to breathe again, and the light came back into her eyes. I had the great honor to hold her hand as she started to smile for the first time since we met, and I am forever honored that I was by her side that moment she chose to *forgive*.

I've never really been as affected by the choices of others, the way that I was with her during that season of my life. I watched her *decide* to forgive, as if she had had a taste of Heaven and knew what she should do to be free. I wasn't a Christian then, but she sure demonstrated more about what a loving God can do then I have ever been taught sitting in a pew. She forgave a world that would understand if she couldn't. She forgave when her tribe told her she should and before I really knew how to forgive what had been done to me or how to forgive myself. She gave herself permission to love herself and carefully guarded the heart of her innocence as it healed, and never entertained any bitterness over all that she had lost.

She was so brave to be forgiving. By forgiving, she set herself free. If *she* can, we can.

I saw that I had a choice then, too. I had to forgive those that hurt me. Most of all, I had to forgive myself for the decisions I had made that led me to a prison cell. I had to stop asking why, and just forgive. I couldn't move forward if I didn't. I couldn't fully become all that I had inside me to be if I stayed bound up in shame and guilt. Shame and guilt are like a rebuff to the freedom God desires for us.

God gives us forgiving hearts, when we can't do it ourselves, He is the source of unlimited forgiveness which we can tap into if we are struggling to forgive.

Let's love ourselves and forgive all our mistakes. The wrong we've done or has been done to us brought us to where we are, yes, but it can be used to walk others to freedom's door. There's so much power in forgiveness! Life and love await us on the other side of our decision to forgive.

Be Brave

Our world has changed. Our Instagram feeds and Facebook pages are full of inspirational posts about being brave and going after our dreams. I love it, but I wonder if we are really *brave*.

Definition of Brave: ready to face and endure danger or pain; showing courage.

Synonyms: courageous, valiant, valorous, intrepid, heroic, lionhearted, bold, fearless, gallant, daring, plucky, audacious.

Are we *really* ready to face and *endure* danger and pain? I'm not so sure, in this *feel*-good type of culture. Do we tell ourselves we will be brave and then at the first hint of discomfort, run back to our comfort zones and promise we will try again *someday*? Do we have what it takes to break bad cycles, push past mediocrity and truly be fearless in the face of adversity?

One danger of today's online world is that we can pretend to be anybody we want to. We post our best pics, share some motivational post about having courage and then go home to a life half-lived, a man we don't respect, or an empty home—*hoping* that our lives will change *somehow*. We camp out on our smartphones, scrolling through, admiring our influencers, patting ourselves on the back for all our likes, and never *really* craft a vision for ourselves, much less make a plan to kick ass and take names.

We want *everyone* to feel brave and valuable and loved and…(fill in the blank) but the reality is, some women will find their face in the mud and just lay there. We can't 'will' them to get up and we can't make a pretty bed for them in the mud because they are *in the fricken' mud!* You *can* carry them for a while. In a sisterhood, when a sister is down, we carry her for a short amount of time, until it's time for her to *decide* to get well. (If we rescue her for too long she won't gain the strength it takes to endure the rest of her journey).

If I catch wind of any women in my residential facilities gossiping about a girl that is struggling, I'll go over there in my damn pajamas if I have to, and wake them up in the middle of the night like it's a boot camp. I will tell them that when we are in a war and your sister is injured, we don't shoot *at* her, that's friendly fire! When she's wounded in the fox hole, we don't leave her there, we go back and get her! We be brave *for* her. We throw her over our shoulder and carry her weight, shoulder her pain. She can't right now, but we can. *We* must be the hero, getting her to safety and not whine, complain or tell a soul about it. *'Be the woman that fixes another's crown without telling the world it was crooked'.* There's a great Facebook quote for ya! At Crossing the Jordan, I'm the General of these women right now and it's my job to get my troops to safety. I'll go in the foxhole, no problem, but our army of women has to learn how to fight *for* each other to grow. I train my troops to be brave, so they can be Generals someday, too.

I know there are some people out there who don't like my training tactics, as I train the women to be vigilant and courageous.
I don't care. Oh, there was a time early on when I cared what
others thought about my methods, so I tried watering it down,
making it softer, and for a minute, against my own best judgment
and experience I made them all *feel* good and stopped pushing
them to any level of discomfort, but guess what happened then?
When a woman relapsed or went back to her abuser or lost her
children because she quit on herself? Those naysayers that crit-
icized my authentic, uncomfortable style *were nowhere to be found.*

We're not truly equipping people when we don't prepare others
to be courageous in the face of fear. Life is hard. Sometimes the
situations are gritty like what I just described but more often than
not, the tragedy is a woman just not living up to her potential,
living a life of perpetual fantasy, dreaming about what she could
have been or could have done or the type of man she wished she
had. It's tragic to stand by and watch her never finishing what she
starts, never making an impact, never finding her purpose and
just wasting away on 'should've-could've-would've's.

I'm not that kind of sister! I'm the girl down in the mud with
women right now, yelling, *Get up! You can do it! You are strong, you
are able, you are brave. Get up and DO IT!*

And when she gets up and starts running, I run *with* her, and the
sisterhood we have built is running with her. We all get tired at
times, because the race is *hard*, but we push each other. We keep
running towards our dreams, and we gain strength from the encouragement we're surrounded by so we can make it across the
finish line. Some women won't be brave, and some women will

never live their best life, but how we show up for them and ourselves matters.

Be Patient

I used to hate it when someone told me to be patient, still do sometimes. Who wants to hear that? No matter how you slice it, waiting mostly sucks. It means you can't get what you want *when* you want it, until it's the 'right time'. It's supposed to be a simple formula: if you wait patiently, then you get what you want. That's supposed to be good news, but it doesn't feel like it.

It *is* mostly good news, though! I mean, if we break it down, in theory, if we are patient we *can get anything we want*. I just don't think we consciously make that connection, especially when we're young. Time is funny when we are under 30, it moves so much slower or we are just in this more hurried state to get what we want and where we want to go as soon as it occurs to us.

The irony is, is that if we aren't patient, we likely won't get there in the time we wanted to anyway, because *there are lessons that need learning along the way that are the keys to entering the place we want to be.* If we skip them by being impatient, and miss out on the lessons, well, sorry, but we can't *stay* there, because *we won't have the tools to maintain the place that we arrived at.* Follow me?

I went to prison. It's not cool, and I made that mistake, but God ended up using what was meant for evil for good, as He always does. That's the short answer. The long answer is there were lessons I needed to learn that I didn't understand at the time. I tried to skip them—and suffered through all the consequences—until I realized that I was stuck, truly stuck, until I surrendered to the process of wisdom. Clearly, in prison I wasn't going anywhere, but you can still escape your purpose in prison, so I had to choose to embrace the lessons or stay stuck in that place in life.

There were a few things that happened in prison that proved the lessons were starting to sink in and serve me well. I was getting stronger and gaining wisdom so I chilled out on the 'being in a hurry' thing and made it my duty to study delayed gratification and 'longsuffering' (having or showing patience despite troubles, especially those caused by other people). There are two paths of growth through pain we can take: one path avoids pain and delays growth indefinitely and the other embraces pain and delays pleasure for a greater purpose. This is the road less-traveled.

I decided to mentally and emotionally train myself to really learn the lesson once and for all, suffering as long as it took, so I didn't have to repeat the lesson. I gave myself a visual: when I sensed a struggle coming, or anticipated pain or heartache, I visualized a storm in the distance. Knowing I would have some work to do to make it through the storm, I would hunker down, mentally and emotionally 'battening down the hatches' to prepare myself for any discomfort, and to not be reaction-driven. I would remind myself the storm will *indeed* pass and I will be grateful when the sun shines again. I would not try to escape it, or make any decisions during that emotional time. I would also find safe shelter through the storm with prayer and surrounding myself with good people that care for me.

There were times during those five years in prison that I did truly suffer in ways that made me wonder if I would make it one more day, but I sensed in my spirit that those times were also preparing me for something so much bigger. I got the vision for Crossing the Jordan a few months after arriving in prison, but I never really comprehended then how much of an impact it would make on so many lives, so at the time I just purposed in my heart and had faith that my pain would serve me in the future somehow, and it did. When we acknowledge and maturely embrace that suffering can be turned around and used as a powerful tool to propel us to the kind of life we desire, even making an impact on the world for good, it makes it easier; even worth going through. That positive outlook that anticipates a good result allows us to perceive the pain as a useful training tool instead of just being a victim of our circumstances, making the journey smoother with less discomfort.

Be patient and choose to take the road less traveled. It's what leaders do, and how dreams are manifested.

Be Humble

Humility and I have rumbled a time or two. I'm embarrassed to say that I had never even heard of the word humility by the time my life fell apart. I'm serious. I'm sure my parents tried to introduce me to the concept, but I never actually heard the word *humility* spoken before.

Without knowing the true definition of the word, the first time I heard it I misunderstood its meaning. After being so broken by a man my first response was to resist anything sounding remotely like weakness. I misunderstood the difference between meekness and weakness, as well, so when I was asked to be humble and meek it got my hackles up, because I equated meek with weak and humility with surrendering, and I *had* to fight, after being passive for so long. I felt too exposed, too bloodied, too spiritually parched, that I instinctively had a fight-or-flight response to everyone and everything. Feeling so low, so insecure in who I was as a woman, I had super-thin skin and would overreact if someone hurt me, and when people tried to help me I would resist out of a false sense of pride. Like a malnourished, worn-out soul, I was hunched over in my infirmities with no strength in my being, pushing people away or repelling them.

Until humility saved me.

When I stopped reacting defensively and learned the actual definition and value of humility, I learned how to live loving others. As a humble person, to be wholly and completely who I was, without feeling pressure to be perfect, I could strive to be the best version of myself.

Part of humility is a culture of honor: giving credit, appreciation and affirmation when it's due. Humility taught me to believe the best in others, that yielding to others selflessly is honorable, not weak. That I could be last, and not first, on *purpose*, for the sake of lifting others up, enjoying their successes along with them. I discovered the pure joy in allowing others to stand on my mighty shoulders, not so they could beat me or pass me on the ladder of success but so I could help them climb to the next level, secure in knowing I have the strength to pull myself up or ask for help if I wanted to.

Humility is remembering we don't know it all, and that *anyone*, from the least to the greatest, oldest to the youngest, can teach us something we need. Humility is knowing we can always improve, so we stay teachable no matter who or where the source of wisdom comes from. Humility is knowing you're the most powerful woman in the room but never having to say it because everyone already knows it. Humility is power, not for the purpose of being better than, but for using your strength to help others to win. It's the opposite of arrogance. Recognizing that everyone brings a necessary piece to the puzzle, and appreciating that fact in advance, humility lets us respect and honor one another.

Humility and I are close friends now. If you haven't met, I am happy to make the introduction. Get to know humility.

Be Open

What does it mean to be open? Kind of obvious, right? 'Be open-minded', we hear this a lot. I've seen far too many people get in trouble, thinking they were open-minded but were instead empty-minded, so they were easily swayed, used, or manipulated by the newest fad, religion, trend, guy, job or whatever led them off course. I caution you to guard your mind, because it's where the battle of our thoughts begins. It's our job to protect our minds.

During conflict, we want to stay open-minded. When I position myself to be open-minded during a conflict, I imagine myself sitting across from the person, entering the conversation with my hands open (not defensively, willing to listen in love and peace) instead of clenching my fists for a fight. Humility honors them by being courteous and open enough to receive why the person has conflict and how we can resolve it. Meekness chooses to build the bridge between us, to make peace.

Being humble keeps us teachable and not defensive. Defensive people can't learn, they're closed off. Pride shuts down their minds and stunts their growth, effectively making them stuck in place, indefinitely. Being open-minded keeps us available to new info and perspectives and seeing people in a different light. Meekness (which is not weakness, it's power under control) doesn't have time for offense, it lets things roll off our backs and sees the opportunity to seek reconciliation. All three of these things: humility, openness and meekness, keeps us light on our feet, easy to pivot, allowing blows to glance off when they come and letting us decide if we must hit back or hug instead. It lets us gain wisdom from every resource, even if it's a child or someone we don't like or whom we don't politically agree with. If a person crosses our path and we stay open to what they have to give, that is our opportunity to learn from them in that moment. Let's not miss out!

Guard your mind while you stay open-minded, being teachable and unoffendable, no matter who it is.

Be Aware

I'm sure there are extraordinarily successful women reading this book, so I want to be careful to not come across as if I assume all my readers are a miserable, lonely, unprepared and entitled mess of a woman. Hey, if you woke up this morning and put your feet on the floor to take one more crack at this thing called life, heck, you're good in my book.

The thing is…is that as good as you can be? Do you desire greatness? Do you have a hunger for more, no matter where you are on the ladder to success? Some don't. Many do. Few make it happen.

Often, when we first start our journey to change, we are *heavy*—in mind, body and soul, lugging ourselves around just to make it through the day. Some days are high-performing and some we barely make it through. Why? What is it that hinders our performance? What is the *thing* that is causing our depression, our heaviness, our unfulfillment, our inaction?

To me, the first step into greatness is *awareness*. Awareness, like openness, go hand in hand on the road to success. They're both driven by curiosity. Most of us think we are already aware of our current reality, but awareness is to *critically observe your thought life, question where the thoughts come from, and then decide if we want to own that thought or shift in another direction.* Awareness is the discipline to think about what you are thinking about. If we don't become aware of our thinking patterns, how can we train our mind to do something different?

Change comes from changing thinking. In my experience, many people are just cruising through life on habits (often bad ones) and routine. Like driving a car. Have you ever gotten in the car with a specific destination in mind but suddenly found yourself going along your normal route instead? It was because your brain created a habit, and once you stopped being aware, it took you there on autopilot.

Our entire lives can easily be on autopilot because it's 'just the way I've always done it.' Becoming aware—'waking up' to your thoughts, patterns, belief systems, and cultural influences—*disrupts that mindlessness.* You can hear your inner thought-life like never before. It's like you've been watching TV your whole life, living in someone else's story. Shut off the TV of your mind, let it get still and quiet, listen to your own breath and thoughts and ask yourself some crucial questions, *who am I, what am I doing, or where am I going?*

Meditation gives us the time and quiet to be with ourselves, our thoughts, and, hopefully, invite God into the conversation, while disinviting the rest is the world, until we've sorted out any bad belief systems or patterns of thought that have negatively influenced our choices and state of mind for years. Often, once we begin to pay attention to our own thoughts, it begins the process of changing them. Then we can free our minds to reprogramming better thinking patterns, and then habits, for ourselves.

Many of the most influential bad habits are the subtlest. Cigarettes or overeating are obvious ones, easy to notice on the outside. But bad habits start in the mind. We could catch ourselves in the habit of sizing up and comparing ourselves with every woman that passes us. That is a bad habit we might not be so aware of, and worse, we may never realize the impact it has on our daily lives. It does! That comparison, as subtle as it may be, may have led to us to feel unworthy, which led to us not taking care of ourselves, which then led us to meeting and accepting an unprepared man who happened to just say all the right things, until one day we wake up sleeping next to an abusive boyfriend wondering how in the hell we got there!

Until we begin to intentionally examine our thought life, we can't move forward. It's like we are trying to fix our car by repairing the dents and ignoring the engine. Until we become aware of what we are up against, that the *engine of our life is our mind*, we will have no idea what to fix.

I had no idea how much I was judging my own daughter. I love Chelsea with a passion that oozes out of me, but I found myself butting heads with her constantly. She wouldn't listen to me. She pushed me away, even though I had 'all the answers' and 'knew better' so she should have learned from me. I...I...I...*I* was the problem. I was so desperate for her life to be perfect because I had put her through so much that I had forgotten the *gift of learning that comes from our mistakes*. I was a big fat hypocrite. I was teaching this stuff to women and yet was so unaware of my own thoughts and behaviors.

I went to a training and found myself complaining to the trainer about Chelsea.

"Why don't you just *be* with her in it?" the trainer asked.

"Excuse me, I am! I love her. I would do anything for her," I snapped.

"Except stop judging her," he snapped sweetly back. Ouch. I just became *aware* of how I wasn't being *with* her.

But that answer seemed too simple. I was more mature than to be missing this simple piece with her, right? *What?! That's stupid.* I was irritated. *There had to be more to it than just be with her.*

"But if I be with her that means I agree with her," I argued.

"Who said that?" he said matter-of-factly, "are you putting words in my mouth?"

"No," I responded.

"Yes, you are. You've made up your mind that being *with* her in her life decisions means approving of all her actions. I mean, gosh, you were in prison at her age. Kind of crazy you can't just *be* with her. She's an adult now, isn't she? Seems like she's doing pretty good to me."

I glared at him. He was kind and wonderful and *right* and I wanted to punch him in his face. I had no idea I was thinking this way. I believed, sincerely, I was trying to guide her, keep her from danger. I sincerely was unaware of my hypocrisy. Trust me, the universe will make sure you can walk out the advice you're dishing out.

That's why it's taken me 20 years of training myself to write this today. I had to be qualified to teach you these things. I had been doing to Chelsea what my mother had done to me...and I was losing her.

How frustrating was it that I could help so many women but my own daughter didn't want to hear my wisdom? I'm the real talk girl, I teach women to listen to their tribe and appreciate their wisdom, but I had become unaware of my own pattern I had created. I was able to cheer the women in my life on, but I was in a desperate place with my daughter, for fear of her becoming me. My approach was the problem. The women I train *invite me* into their space and lives to help them. Chelsea had *not* invited me. I was trying to shove it down her throat...and like a willful toddler, she was spitting it right back in my face.

I shifted that moment as I became aware. It was easy, too, after so many years of hard work. I think it was easy because I wanted results, not just to be right anymore. I imagined what good could happen between us if I took the trainers' advice and just showed up; no advice, no agenda, praying for an invitation from Chelsea but willing to wait however long it took.

I'm ecstatic to say everything has changed since that day. Chelsea is my best friend and comes to me about EVERYTHING, the little and the big things. The change in my attitude didn't come immediately but she noticed the shift right away.

"What's up, mom? Somethings different with you," she'd say.

I would just smile and say, "Nothing girl. How was your day?"

Chelsea would smile back. She knew me well enough to know I was intentionally doing something different in our relationship, but she didn't know what and she didn't mind. We had peace.

It didn't take but a few months before she began ask me for advice. The first couple of times, I was jumping up and down in the house, hand over the phone, pointing to it, whispering crazily to Michael, "Oh my God, it's Chelsea, calling *me* for advice!"

Michael would laugh and shoot me a thumbs up, celebrating every little breakthrough. It had been a long road, but my openness and awareness allowed me to break a generational pattern that had gone on between us mothers and daughters for far too many years.

Bravely become aware of what you are thinking, as it's the first step to renewing your mind...and *changing your life.*

Be Responsible

Imagine each of these subjects in this chapter as stepping stones in a path, one after the other, each as important as the other to get you where you want to go.

To take responsibility for the actions in your past requires you to forgive and be aware and be humble and not defensive. These are all parts of the growth and healing process. We can't walk into greatness—have a good man, live a life of excellence and take responsibility for our future—while still being a victim of our past.

Taking ownership of our mistakes is important so we don't repeat them. If we can't take responsibility for and own the crap we've done, we *aren't mature enough to get the kind of life we want, or even handle it if we could.*

178

True, extreme ownership is reserved for the great leaders, the mighty men and women of this world, who humbly admit where they missed it and take responsibility for it *and* for those they lead. You can't be the relationship manager if you don't own it. You can't be a successful executive without the responsibility that comes with it. If your team fails, the crap rolls *uphill*. If you don't take the steering wheel of your own life, you don't get to complain about who is driving, how they're driving, and where you end up.

I know that I am going to piss off quite a few domestic violence advocates, here, but you know what, *I could have left* that son of a b**ch abuser. I was with him of my own free will. For so many years, I said there was no way I could leave, that he'd chase me and torture me, and he did. Yet I had the capability to leave, so it was still *my choice* to stay, and I did because I didn't want to do the hard work it took to change my life, even if it would be better. It was easier to come up with a thousand reasons why I was a victim, and stay that way. People believed my excuses because of the level of violence I endured but I STAYED. I *STAYED*. There's no way around that…and once I *owned* it, somehow I became a new woman.

No one made me use drugs or commit crimes, either. *There are millions of people that have had horrible things done to them, too, yet many choose a good path with honor.* I didn't. I tapped out. Many people spend their lives serving others, in more ways that I ever will and they have gone through way worse than I have. I had no excuse, really. I was hurt, yes, but there was another path I could have chosen. When I broke the events down in my head and admitted this to myself, I was able to get up off the ground and finally fight for my life.

I live a powerful life because I take responsibility for my past, my present, my future, my team, my marriage, my place in the community and my contribution to my country. When I do, I also honor those who've contributed to my life. We must be brave and willing to face the hard work that comes from taking extreme ownership, but it's a life well lived. The load is *heavy* at times. However, I draw strength from God and lean on Michael and my team when I'm weary. Walking in ownership is still easier and lighter than crawling through life burdened as a pathetic victim of our own circumstances. We're better than that. *You* are made for more than that. Don't stay in the lazy mind trap, let's own our lives. Be responsible.

Be Creative

I think many of us miss this one completely and are surprised how it affects our lives as a whole. When I was young the phrase 'being creative' wasn't used the way it is these days. I literally thought creative people only meant artists, makers (people who made things), and fashion designers. I remember wanting to be a fashion designer when I was 10 but I couldn't get used to the sewing machine so I gave up. I tried to learn macramé and knitting from my mother—sucked at that, too. I took art classes, ballet, was in several community plays and tried to sing, all to my parents' embarrassment. I just kept trying and failing. Can't say that I felt like a failure, though, because I really didn't *like* to do any of these things. I wanted to like them but I just couldn't. I was craving *something* but didn't know what.

One day, some guy said to someone else in front of me, "Talk about creative, Dana is the most creative women I have ever met!"

"What?! Me?!" I replied, shocked. I had never heard anyone say anything like that about me!

He looked at me like I was crazy. He was confused that I didn't know that about myself.

"Yes, you," he continued, "You are always coming up with new, creative ideas. You're always trying to improve the spaces you are in or start a new business out of nothing. You see things for their *potential* and how you can make them more beautiful. Your ideas never stop. That's creative."

I felt like breaking out into a cartwheel. I wanted to shout *I knew it! I knew I was creative!*

Instead I smoothly replied, "Wow, thank you! What a nice compliment."

The little girl in me was excited, though, so when I got home I googled it. Google then wasn't what it is today, but I still got a sense that 'being creative' was more than the box I had put it in. To be creative, by definition, is to relate to or involve the use of the imagination or original ideas to create something, anything. *What the heck?* I sat back, stunned. *I'm creative!* Sounds a little basic writing about it here now, but for me it was just this beautiful amazing discovery.

The way we express ourselves is our contribution to the world. That's me being creative. I'm being creative with you, right now. Being creative is risky, yes, but when we face our fear and tell fear, *I am going to be myself and express myself in my own unique way, no matter what*, it's like we grow wings to fly. We become *alive*. We develop our own personal language with the universe. We get to leave our personal mark on the world. Our days become exciting, fulfilling and we can't wait to get out of bed in the morning.

I believe all of us are creative in some way, and when we don't get to express that creativity, we become pressure cookers, ready to blow. When we release our creativity, we become poetic painters of the world, each adding our unique strokes to the canvas of life. It looks different for each of us. When we let that creative part of ourselves breathe, live and imagine freely, our problems become smaller, our relationships become *better*. We aren't staring at what we don't have, we are imagining something wonderful into existence!

Be creative. Do what freely and wonderfully expresses yourself, whatever that may be. Unfold your wings and fly.

Be Productive

It's interesting, transitioning the conversation from creativity to being productive. Creation feels freeing while production feels constraining (compelling, obligating), at least to me, at first glance. I'm a bit of a workhorse, so I had more of a hard time giving myself permission to create rather than produce. I like results, so being productive really turns me on!

The thing was, I wasn't *truly productive*. I thought I was, but it was fluff, busy-ness, hot air disguised as production. Being active or busy does not mean you are productive, I learned this the hard way. I *like feeling* productive, so I did a lot of things and yes, there was evidence of a positive result, but I wasted TOO much time during the process. It felt like I was spinning my wheels at times, but I didn't want to admit it. Pride, I guess. When I really looked at how unproductive I was, it was right around the time we had built a successful social enterprise, so obviously no one would accuse me of not being productive, surrounded by the evidence that we produced and delivered daily, as it were.

What I learned, just me alone in my office, is that I had a pattern of ping-ponging: starting a creative project then bouncing to starting another one before the first one was completed, then starting *another* project (with at least 20 windows open on my computer at a time), thus slowing down all the projects' completion time. Now I recognize that these were gold-plated problems at this point in my life, but remember, I was shooting for greatness, not mediocrity, here.

Many people could have the life they want if they learn to 'plan to work, and work the plan', as a friend shared with me once. We don't move the needle fast because of procrastination or a lack of actual productivity, which then increases our chance of failure because when you don't see results early on, it's hard to stay motivated.

If we are intentional about planning to produce results then we won't lose interest, if we keep producing, that is. We can only fake it so long before the evidence suggests that we are 'fluffing it' as I call it: making it seem like we are producing much when we really aren't at all. We are so much better than that!

If our focus is on creating the life we desire, then we must (and should naturally) produce results. When we are productive, the good man (or job!) will come *to* us because they will be interested in us, as we will naturally attract them. And if we keep being productive, that good man, boss or team will *stay* because we *keep* them interested.

Billionaires and beggars alike have the same 24 hours in a day. Like us, they must choose how to spend their time. Read books on successful habits and how to be more productive. Watch You-Tube videos and listen to podcasts. Join a mastermind group. GET productive.

I used to believe that transformation had to come from the inside out until one day in a class Sarah said that if we change our *environment* first, that can cause a *shift inside* us which we respond to by changing. Try it: clean your house, paint your walls, wash your car, file your paperwork, don't let the mail pile up, open it, get your life in order. Face whatever it is you are avoiding head on and you will find the outward production will cause an inward shift to produce more.

I made a habit of doing the things I least like *first* when I get into the office every day. I don't let myself do the enjoyable, creative stuff until the things I'm avoiding get done. When I used to think I was productive, I was actually just spending a ton of energy avoiding things. Now, they're at the top of my do-to list and I get them done first thing every day.

Michael and I both get up at 4:30am so we can have quality time together before going to the gym. Then we meet back at home for a quick kiss and some coffee before we go to work. I always have headphones on, listening and learning and he always has his head in a Kindle reading and learning. We produce naturally because we care, because what we accomplish impacts others. Time *does* matter. It doesn't have to feel like pressure but let's be clear: time ticks by and our daily production is the critical active part of building the life we want, moving from fantasy to fact, from dreaming to doing, from existing to living abundantly.

People are counting on you to be efficient and your family is counting on you to run at your optimal pace. Just start, right where you are.

Be Attractive

Seems simple, huh? Just...*be attractive*. When I say it so matter-of-factly, I am aware of how easily this could offend. 'Be attractive and get the guy.' It sounds shallow, but—

Why deny this simple truth?

Men have a natural urge to mate with beautiful women. Long thick hair, nice skin, curves in the right places, breast size and hip size are all signs of a healthy woman to procreate with. From a biological perspective, men want the same thing that women want, to advance their genes. When I looked at 'being attractive' from this perspective, it boiled down to simple biology—which I could absorb without taking it personally as rejection—when a man did not find *me* attractive.

The reality is that there are times in our lives when we are not 'attractive'. 'Being attractive' goes beyond appearance, it extends to how we 'self-care': that includes our career, home, vehicle, our desire to learn, emotional health, our ambition and drive to succeed, our children, our spouses—really every single aspect of our lives. If we live a sloppy life, it shows up everywhere. Not being the optimal version of ourselves affects who or what we attract in every area of our lives.

Those times I was unattractive, I wasn't *attracting* the men that I was *attracted* to. Attractive men (physically fit and well cared for) would not pursue me when I was not taking care of myself (being attractive). Out of rejection and loneliness, I would compromise and go after a less attractive man. Was that a wise choice? Of course not. Why not? Because I wasn't *attracted* to him. I was *settling* because of how I felt about myself.

Now, before you freak out on me, let me explain that I do agree with the body-positive movement and in no way am I saying you are only attractive if you are skinny, have long hair, perfect skin, a big booty, tiny waist and big boobs!

I will say this, though: we had best be careful of the path the radical feminists are taking us down. I don't agree with the 'anything goes' type of body philosophy, either. It's like we are nervous to express that being lean or a healthy weight is good for fear of upsetting the body-positive movement. I am the first to cheer you on towards loving the body you're in but there is a line and we have become an obese nation. Health *matters*. Most of our health issues are, in fact, related to our size. Let's be careful not to swing so far in the other direction that we abandon the benefits of being lean and healthy.

Women, we should be very honest with ourselves. Are you attracted to a certain body type on a man? I follow Jenna Kutcher (check her out on IG). She went viral after being questioned by social media trolls how she could get a husband with a six-pack when she was a full-figured woman. Now, that is just *mean*. I think her story is a good one to follow because Jenna is 'healthy' in all areas of her life, but not *skinny*. You can tell Jenna takes good care of herself. She is a highly successful business women that serves other women in a mighty way and her service and commitment to women makes her *very* attractive. Who she is as a human is *attractive.* She is honest about her body image issues when something comes up, but it doesn't stop her from keeping the other areas of her life attractive, well-kept and moving forward. Jenna is stylish, confident, kind, brave, and open; at least what one experiences from her podcasts and how she presents herself to the world. Therefore, she married a hot guy that adores her because she knows who she is and walks boldly in it, sharing her insecurities and being real with her struggles. This is what attractive looks like.

As a women's advocate, I love that the message that we are 'enough' is getting out there. We are more than enough...but that doesn't give us a license to be entitled, unkept, lazy, and still expect to get our dream man. Laziness and entitlement make a bad combination. We can *try* but we will not get the results we really want, and we will end up being 'enough' alone at home or with a man we just settled for.

It is risky to say all this, as it's in direct opposition to the messages we get in the media. Those messages are subtle but dangerous. We need to be very careful of the messages we are sending our daughters. High-value driven men are and will continue to be attracted to well-kept healthy and *attractive* women (with attractive meaning more than the weight on the scale). We don't want our daughters to have to settle for less, so let's not stick our heads in the sand and pretend this is not true. No woman should settle. We all should shoot for excellence, physically and emotionally, within ourselves and our mates. Let's improve our messaging, look in the mirror, and strive to *be* our best, to *get* the best.

I've mentored countless women that seem totally clueless why they can't find a good man. I'm like, *when was the last time you got a haircut? Why are you wearing frumpy-pajama looking outfits to work? Why is your style ten or twenty years behind the current fashion? When was the last time you had a makeover?*

Yes, being attractive *is* about our appearance *and it isn't*: its about *way* more than just our appearance. It's how we care for the look of our home, how we decorate our office, the style and fit of our clothes, our makeup, our hair color and style, our teeth, our facial expression, our hands, feet, and nails, our posture, our faith, our positivity, how well-kept and well-behaved our children are and how we present ourselves to a room full of people. Our entire being and life should be attractive if we desire to attract a good man. Girl, it's just what's up. We have to exude a spirit of excellence if we want an excellent existence. If you want to be mediocre, put the book down and just settle, but at least be honest with yourself. Or be *brave* and go for it! Just don't pretend you don't know why you aren't getting results, anymore. We usually know why anyways, it's just painful to admit it. We see our inadequacies in the mirror, and our lives testify when we are not living up to our potential. We'd just rather complain in self-pity than do what it takes to change.

The good news is that you are beautifully and wonderfully made, gloriously designed by God. Choose to see yourself that way, align with His vision of you, and take steps towards His vision for your life. When we seek truth, the truth sets us free. We are no longer chained by the lies we have told ourselves.

During the push to start the nonprofit, we weren't taking very good care of ourselves. Fueled by energy drinks, we worked countless hours. I remember a defining, compromising moment of choice I made. I looked in the mirror, saw the weight packing on, saw it all clearly and *gave myself permission to live in sweats and a ponytail* until Crossing the Jordan was a reality.

Thirty pounds later, I was feeling miserable and that 'martyr to the cause' story that I had excused myself with was threatening to implode. That false humility frankly made me feel ugly inside and out. My home life was suffering, too, and I had a lot of really good excuses. I mean, sacrificing myself for others is noble of me, right?

One day Michael and I were walking together downtown, and he looked handsome that day. I saw a group of women coming towards us look at him and one of the women tried to catch his eye. He looked away immediately.

"Did that woman just give you *the look?*" I asked.

"Yep."

"Do women actually give you that look often?" I pushed.

"Yep."

"Are you serious?"

"Gee, thanks a lot." Michael smiled back at me.

"Wow, she was pretty hot," I congratulated, "Good job."

Michael loves that frankness about me and even as disgusting as I felt in that moment compared to those women, my confidence was able to trump my insecurity, thankfully. Michael knew it was just a season of sacrifice and pushing hard for both of us, so he forgave the lack of effort I made on myself. We had both let ourselves go a bit, but men are just allowed more grace in this area. However, I was not in denial about my current appearance, and the 'mistresses' were circling, so I knew it was time I better get my groove back.

Remember, I've never been the jealous type. It's kind of weird, so I just consider it a gift from God and won't take the credit… but I woke up that day. I went out to dinner with some graduates of our program and afterwards took a selfie with them. I literally didn't recognize the woman in that picture that night. But it was me…and I was shocked how I looked. I had never been that heavy in my entire life, and most of all, so sloppy and unkept. I certainly wasn't living by my marital motto, *always be as hot as the mistress would be.*

The next day I led a 90-day weightloss contest within our program and dropped 30 pounds. I started walking through the malls for inspiration to get my style vibe back. My oldest daughter said she wouldn't speak to me until I grew out my bangs, so I went to my hairstylist for a modern makeover. I started getting my makeup done regularly at MAC and bought the products they suggested. (I saved money on food, so I used it to buy quality products). I asked my daughters to give me advice about my style until I had my groove fully back.

"Oh girl, look at you," Chelsea started saying when I would visit her, so I knew I was back on my game. Both of my daughters never hold back so I trust their authenticity. Both had been warning me that I wasn't living up to my own advice (I had trained them well) and finally their accountability with me popped the martyr bubble I'd been floating around in.

I'll tell you this, though, I won't ever let myself go, again. Ever. Why? Because I have created this wonderful life where I am expected to be on my game. I have surrounded myself with women that are in constant forward motion. I've developed trainings and an environment that require me to constantly be ready, publicly. I've designed this dream life that has no Plan B. I've torched the ships that could sail me back to settling for anything less than best. I've crossed myself to the point of no return, only excellence. I chose to be the face of our brand, by design—it's been the ultimate accountability—and you know what? When I did, our brand grew. People respect and relate to someone who has done what she preaches.

You want total transformation? Burn the ships, as Michael says. Remove every possible escape route. Put yourself *way* out there. When you get haters make them your motivators. You will be judged for the risks you're taking, but guess what, people judge you no matter what you do, don't they? So press on.

I still have people question me if my transformation is a sign of insecurity. So, what, I got a boob job and Botox, does that mean I am shallow? Nope. It just means that after my weight loss, my boobs shriveled away and after laying in the sun with Crisco in the 90's and some past drug use, I needed some Botox. I don't care what people think because I know if they could, they *would* get work done, too. Everyone's a critic until they are presented with the same set of circumstances or choices and then, *suddenly*, people understand your decisions. So forget the haters and *be kind to yourself.*

We've established that good men are hard to find and that we are not entitled to one just because we *want* one. The other harsh reality is that *if there is a small pool of good men, then the numbers are not in our favor,* not anymore. I am in no way saying that we should compete in any way that would be dishonorable to another woman, I am simply stating a reality. We had better be wise enough to acknowledge the cold hard fact that we need stay on our game to heighten our chances for success.

Listen, all this stuff about looking good is hard to deliver to you because I want you to feel encouraged, not bad about yourself. I just refuse let you stay in your old stretchy sweats and whine about not being loved! *Toss the granny panties! Burn them!* Get radical and *feel alive.* You are beautiful to start with! I believe that to be true. Does your current version of you align with the vision that you have for *yourself?* If so, great! Yes, there are gorgeous women in gorgeous sweats out there, but we can at least get some nice ones and show the world we are *working on* living a life of power and purpose.

Beauty is in the eye of the beholder. I like Michael big and muscular, with a little meat around his waist. (It makes me feel tiny). Most men like women a little curvy. We all have different preferences, just don't ignore your current condition. This part might not be written for you because you already look like a supermodel. Some of you just have a horrible, bratty attitude that needs fixing. That's not attractive, either!

Some women have a hippy vibe and I love that. Just make sure you brush your damn hair and get your teeth cleaned regularly. There's a way to keep ourselves up, even if we're broke. Some women prefer conservative appearances but make sure you aren't so uptight that you look half dead. You can be modest *and* alive. Some women are sexy but pull your damn skirt down, that's not sexy, it's slutty, and you don't want the man who is looking for slutty. Sista, I have dressed every version of the above and let me tell you, your vibe will attract the same vibe and the type of man you will spend the rest of your life with. Dress less; get less. You will attract the quality that you dress. Dress quality; get quality. Your outward appearance is your first impression. If you want a high-performance life, make it a memorable one.

Try not to compare yourself to other women, however. And don't ever be jealous, it will eat you alive, and it's one of the quickest ways to push a good man out of your arms and into another's. Instead compete against *yourself*. Bless the women in your life that are super-hot and on fire. We really do rise by lifting others up. I have plenty of gorgeous women in my life that have super-hot bodies and a bunch of money. So, what? I cheer them on and sometimes challenge them, in a good sisterly way, to up *their* game, because I love to inspire and expect the best from people.

What we focus on grows. I make it my business to stay attractive, always being open to change, and always striving to be my own best version of myself. But that version is different for everyone. Get in touch with your persona (how you present yourself to the world) how you walk into a room, and how you impact others with your attitude and energy. Is it a good vibe or a bad vibe?

You can look at yourself in the mirror, be content, and still push to be better. I want you to live great adventures and have radical life experiences. I don't want you to look at Instagram travel posts and wish you had a body like hers to go to tropical paradises like that. I want you to reinvent yourself, train hard and go anywhere in the world you want to go with the man of your dreams. You're dreaming of it anyway, so just start! I am. If I can come out of the pits of hell and reinvent myself, anybody can. It starts with faith and then it's about retraining the way you think.

Think that you are attractive, and you will start to be. Love yourself. Love every flaw, embrace what you can't change and then change what you can. Time *is* ticking, no matter what the dreamers say. The difference between a dreamer and a doer is the action that accompanies your vision, so take action, reinvent yourself, be a doer. Let your beauty shine.

Be Healthy

In light of discussing our outer appearance, I want to talk for a minute about our physical health. How do you really feel, physically? Are you able to move well, sleep well, and maintain your energy and focus? Maybe you are in great shape and want to skip this part, but I know there are so many of us that have limited knowledge on the impact our internal health has on our lives. I believe the habits that we have for the way we eat, what we eat, and how we move are the most critical part of the transformation process. How we treat our body affects our attractiveness, our mental stability and our emotional health in such a way that if we focus on being 'healthy', most of the other things follow.

For instance, I had no idea how cortisol was affecting my life. Cortisol is a stress hormone that is released when we are under pressure. I learned that it often leads to belly fat, not to mention Alzheimer's. I used to think that busyness was some sort of badge of honor and when someone said I looked tired, I'd reply "I'll sleep when I'm dead." Ok...but I didn't want to look dead! Then I learned about cortisol, started going to bed earlier, weight started to fall off, and my face looked better and younger.

I thought Splenda was good for me (because equal was bad) and then I had to switch to Organic Stevia because I learned Splenda was telling my body to store fat. I lost 6 pounds immediately when I quit consuming Splenda all day.

There are so many ways that I have shifted, with little effort, to a healthier lifestyle. I google everything, all the time, and I kept studying and learning because I didn't know what I was doing was wrong, but I sure knew I didn't like how I was aging. I started to claim I'm going to age backwards. The Botox helped! Then I learned about autophagy through fasting. When you fast, you release HGH into your system and it's pretty much the fountain of youth. People can't believe how much younger I look now but it's because I got healthy in a radical, non-mainstream way, through a fasting lifestyle.

When I wanted to shift the direction of our company, I knew it was going to take me being very focused and alert, so I cut out carbs (which fogged my brain) and I started to train six days a week at a small gym that held me accountable. You want to know what else I do sometimes that no one knows? I will put the Rocky movie theme song (Eye of the Tiger) in my headphones as I run fast down the street. I'll play it in my mind as I walk in my dress and heels from the car in the parking garage to my corner office. I *plan* to win. I get my head in the game every single morning. I meditate on scriptures and I journal, writing down my dreams and then making a list to make them a reality.

Our health is physical, mental and emotional, and if we are careful what we put into our bodies and minds, it helps us create the outcome we desire. Our brains are supercomputers that do what we tell it to. I'm no 'Rocky' or 'The Rock' for that matter but as I write to you now, I'm training to cut every pound of fat off me to get ripped at age 46. Why? Because I mentor women that trade one addiction for another, food for drugs, when they first get clean, so when they see me do what seems impossible, they can up their game as well. *The way you live your life is the greatest advice you'll ever give.*

Get healthy and watch every area of your life transform.

Be Dedicated

To be dedicated means to be devoted to a task or purpose; having single-minded loyalty or integrity. Synonyms are: committed, firm, steadfast, resolute, unwavering, loyal, faithful, true.

We must anchor ourselves to this process because that is what it takes to transform. Because change can be painful sometimes or discouraging when we aren't getting the results we want at first, we tend to be disloyal to our own commitment. It's so easy to renegotiate the terms we made for ourselves, especially if we don't have our sisterhood for accountability. I mean, who will really know if you give up on your commitment to transform? YOU WILL!

Even when we just tell ourselves we are going to do something and don't, no matter how small that 'thing' is*, we psychologically register it as a failure when we don't follow through or complete it.* I figured this out early on in my transformation. I felt and saw the devastation in a person's life when they didn't keep their word to themselves or to others.

When I decided to do whatever it took to change, I realized, with incredulity, that my life had become a mess simply through a *series of broken commitments*! Really, it was that simple. I had big dreams, in great detail, and often I knew the first step of action to take, but I still chose not to take it. Or, I would commit to myself to not be with a man until I knew what a good man was, but with the first sign of attention from a man I went for it—another broken commitment to myself. I would promise my parents I wouldn't use drugs, yet that very night I would relapse. I would commit to eating healthy and then end up at a McDonalds' with friends. I would have one conversation after another with myself about how I would change this or that and the next day, I would fail.

I had created such a pattern of breaking commitments that I was in a constant state of despair. Depressed, I would outwardly blame others that no one believed a word I said while at the same time knowing I had done this to myself. I couldn't keep my word to myself, much less to others. It was a terrible existence. The weight of guilt and the shame of never completing anything or honoring my word totally hobbled me. It all started with one broken promise...then another, and another, one after the other, until my self-esteem was so low I could barely function. Then I simply self-destructed. Looking back, I don't even know when that first broken promise started, probably quite early in my teens. Without comprehending the pattern, I couldn't carry the weight of debt of my mini failures, and they gained compound interest. Then I was buried alive under a mountain of broken promises.

The pattern was broken the day I got arrested. In prison, I had time to reconcile the debt to myself. Gods' and my own forgiveness helped me wipe the slate clean and see the light of day again. To breathe. Then, it was time to stop the endless compromises, to never be buried alive again. It was time to BE DEDICATED. One day I woke up and prayed, "I am not going to lay my head down tonight until I have kept my promises, to others and myself." And that was that. My new life began.

I still live like this today. I keep short accounts and stay in for-giveness. I'm NOT perfect, I make mistakes, but I am committed to making them right, quickly. So much so, at times I have been too blunt with people, or I needed to chill out about how quickly I insisted on resolving an issue, but I am dedicated to never let the guilt or unforgiveness of a broken commitment to myself take root again in my soul.

Here's an example: if I tell myself I won't eat something that day, and I do it anyway, I quickly forgive myself and get back on plan the next day. I recommit. It's a running joke with my tribe, if they see me eating a sweet or a carb, literally all of them say, with a grin, "Back on plan tomorrow?" I'd laugh, "Yup, back on plan tomorrow!" But guess what though? It works. I keep short accounts with myself, so if I fail, I don't let it go another day. I refuse to allow the renegotiating to be a pattern.

I have a plan for keeping short accounts with others, too. I keep a clear conscience. When I hurt someone, I do my utmost to ask forgiveness and make it right by nightfall. I am human, so I can get pissed or miss the mark on occasion, but it is rare, because I am very serious about my 'short accounts' plan. This way of life allows me to be a loyal friend, a good mother, a great trainer and a hell of a wife—because my word means something—and everyone knows it. I'm the friend you want to have because I will do what I say I am going to do. Considering I used to be a total loser, this is a big win for team Dana! This daily commitment to keep my word also allows me to move the needle forward with my measurable goals: I keep anxiety at bay because I focus on 'just today', leaving tomorrow's planning for tomorrow.

Language

When I entered the transformation training world I discovered the next level of living in commitment: language. Language is a critical piece in the transformational process, and I intend to write a lot more on the subject in the future. For now, here's a crash course: have you ever heard the expression *It's not what you say, it's how you say it?* This is true. That expression is so casually used that I do not believe it adequately expresses the true impact that tone and language make in our relationships. How we communicate our feelings, desires and needs can either build a marriage up or tear a family apart. Language is a big deal.

Here is an example:

"Michael! You didn't do the backyard! You promised you would! I am sick of you not doing what you said you would. I'm so pissed right now!" And then the rest of the day pretty much sucks because I started a fight, and I am now wide open for him to counter with a list of my shortcomings.

Instead, try this approach:

The day before I say, "Michael, what day are you committing to do the backyard?"

He says, "On Thursday after work. I'm slammed all week."

"Ok, great. Can I hold you to that promise?" He says yes.

Thursday night comes, and the yard isn't done, and he hasn't said a word.

I say, "Babe, you didn't do that back yard. Do you acknowledge the broken promise?"

He says, "Yup, I sure do. I'll have to get to it on Saturday. Please forgive my broken promise."

I say, "Sure. Thank you for recommitting."

I know, it sounds so formal, *but holy smokes, this works!* I mean, this can save a marriage! It's golden. Now, at this point in your life, this kind of conversation might sound crazy, not realistic or even corny, I get it. Michael and I felt almost silly when we shifted to using this language for the way we commit to things. But the thing is this tool in our marriage created a way to keep the peace, like almost every day of our lives, around issues that would literally tear other families apart. Now even our children operate this way, acknowledging their broken agreements, too, and because of how we 'language' it, they understand the importance of being committed, keeping short accounts, keeping their word, and staying faithful even in the little things.

Dedicating yourself to this type of language will help keep you committed in so many wonderful ways. Otherwise, you can be like a ship tossed by the sea. Dedication and language are like the rudder and the ship's wheel: together, they will take you where you want to go and keep you from crashing on the rocks.

If you are dedicated to transforming your life, keeping short accounts and keeping your word allows you to chunk your commitments into realistic parts, so you can take on change one day at a time. It gives yourself a grace day to shift your approach or the way you communicate, accept responsibility for an error and get back on plan tomorrow. Soon enough your little daily victories grow into huge, monumental triumphs, with accompanying peace of mind.

You get stronger the more you live a dedicated life. Your boss will believe in you or your team will know you can be counted on. Your friends will value your loyalty, your children will know you will always be there for them and your husband will trust you. They are all watching, and they will see you doing the right thing, in all things, one little moment at a time.

This level of integrity spills over into other parts of our lives and nourishes our souls. We become light on our feet and free in our minds because we lay our heads down on our pillows each night having kept our commitments to those we love, and ourselves. Let's be disciplined and dedicated. It's who we *want* to be.

Be Grateful

Over the years, I've really dug deep to get to the root of why Michael and I, against all odds, were able to overcome our addictions, start a rapidly growing Social Enterprise Empire, build the kind of marriage people dream of, and completely transform our lives, in every possible way. What was it about *us*? Why were so many others with similar pasts *unable* to turn their lives around and make the kind of impact we have, on others? I wasn't looking to compare or elevate ourselves, I just wanted to understand what set us apart, as a couple, so I could help others rise above their difficulties, too.

Digging through our pasts as a couple, I unearthed a common thread…*gratitude*. Michael and I never forgot where we came from. Humbly keeping the pain of the past in the front of our minds kept us *grateful*. We don't *live* in the past, we just don't forget it. It reminds us of how far we've come, allows us to have empathy for all those we support, and it lets us keep a perspective of how blessed our lives are now.

After many years of mentoring and training, my experience is that if you are not grateful, transformation is near to impossible. Any change made won't *stick*. Pride and arrogance are both handicapping. Pride makes us blind to where we need to go because we've either forgotten how far we've come or we are unteachable, unmovable, hobbling ourselves because, as a 'know it all' we are no longer open to or appreciative of the input of others. I have watched probably hundreds of people walk right back into the slavery of their old life because they were ungrateful for all they had been given. It's truly the quickest way to sink back down into your old life. Being grateful requires humility and positivity, so if we forget the cost of our journey and don't honor those that have walked the battlefield with us, we are in danger of being taken out. Humility is the shield that protects us from the evils of pride. Empathy for others while having an attitude of gratitude is the greatest weapon we have against the real and present danger of negativity.

When I feel myself getting proud (most leaders struggle with this), I intentionally 'go low'—remind myself of where I came from and how I got here today with the help of others. When I start thinking I have all the answers, that's the first sign I am swimming in dangerous waters. It starts to feel like that lack of gratitude climbs up on you, weighing you down. We might sense something's wrong with our thinking, but we might not catch exactly what the problem is. We can't see the 'pride creep' on ourselves because when it's happening, we are too proud to admit there's something wrong. A trusted tribe can point out the arrogance slithering its way onto you. The best way to shake it off is with *gratitude:* for the tribe that cares enough to hold up a mirror, and for the life we have been given, no matter where we are at today.

Yes, we all have met or heard of wildly successful people that have 'made it' financially that also happen to be arrogant or full of pride. Truly, though, they are miserable humans, unhappy and lonely. To me, that is *not* success, no matter how big your bank account is. Have you ever hung out with someone that constantly complains about their life, always talking about 'someday' this or 'someday' that? These people can't enjoy the journey because they aren't grateful for what they have been given. In fact, the lack of gratitude will cut their journey short, if it happens at all. *A negative attitude is the surest way to stay stuck in one place.*

Ironically, some of my dearest memories are from when I was in prison, jogging in the yard, looking through the double barbed wire fences, thanking God for the day He had given me. That was my 'freedom,' and it was rooted in my gratitude. My appreciation for what I *did* have—the breath in my lungs, my legs to run with, my sisters to lean on—offered me a new perspective apart from my circumstances, allowing me to move joyfully forward with my dreams. I got to be the only prison fitness instructor during those five years. I was allowed to be the first to get released every day from the unit and so most of the women would see me walk the yard to the gym by myself, because no one else was allowed to be out there that early.

Often women would come up to me and ask, "I see you walking, so excited, as if you are in a hurry. Who the heck is in a rush when they have so much time to still do?"

I'd laugh, and say, "I'm on a mission to be my best when I am released. I have some work to do, so I'm doing it!"

Some women got inspired by that attitude of mine and joined my classes, but many women resented how I perceived my time inside. *The only difference I can see between those women that transformed their lives and those that kept coming back to prison was GRATITUDE.* Yes, it's hard to believe gratitude is THAT transformative, THAT powerful of an attitude, but it is. We are given *one life*, so we had better find a way to be thankful for it, no matter where we are, or we are destined to stay stuck in the misery of an ungrateful heart.

Have you ever seen those children on TV playing soccer with a roll of rubber bands or a can? They look so happy, and they *are* because they are enjoying the simple things in life and they're just enjoying that moment of joy. Crossing the Jordan may be opening an orphanage in Kenya, Africa soon. We ship used clothing there now from our resale stores. We have discovered that if we have a nonprofit there, we will not have to pay the 'duty tax' on the container and we can then use that money to fund the orphanage without having to spend an extra dime! Michael leaves for Africa in a few days. We are so excited. It's been a dream of ours to have a mission arm of our nonprofit.

Do you know what one of our main reasons for doing it is? Of course, to help children in Africa, but also to help our residents in America become *grateful*. We plan to send our residents that are close to graduation to the orphanage in Africa to serve, for a main reason: to shift their perspective and help them live in gratitude. Why? *Because we know their chances of success hinge on their ability to have an attitude of gratitude* for the new life they have been given, and to keep that perspective. We *invest in gratitude* because it is *that* valuable, it is like food for the soul. A life that is grounded in positivity and appreciation can withstand any storm and grow even during hard times. A person that appreciates the rain understands that joy comes in the morning.

Be grateful. Never forget how far you've come. Celebrate the milestones and thank those that carried you when you weren't strong. Gratitude will shift you into a place where miracles can happen. It is the power that affects the world around us for good, so nurture it and grow strong in it. And then go carry someone while they are weak, reminding them of how sweet the journey is and how to keep pressing on because it's worth it.

Take a Stand

If we don't stand for something, we will fall for anything.

This quote is one of my favorites of all time. It makes me feel like a warrior just saying it. The coolest thing these days is that I embody this in my everyday life. But there was a day I *would* fall for anything. Especially some idiot guy throwing me some 'game' just to get me in bed. Ugh, those days were lame and embarrassing to admit.

I've clearly always been mouthy so when I felt strongly about something, I wasn't quick to fold. I was prideful and stubborn. I'm not even sure that I knew what I *did* stand for morally, socially, or politically. (Speaking of which, I won't discuss politics here because we, as women, don't know how to have a healthy debate and still love each other anymore, which totally ticks me off). For the sake of sisterhood, I won't express what I stand for on the tough subjects that are dividing our nation even though you can probably guess or stereotype me and get half of it right.

Let's just be sisters first, because if we are, we might actually stand more unified.

I'd like to talk about the 'system' for a minute: a set of principles or procedures according to which something is done; an organized scheme or method. In this context, by system I mean our prevailing social order. Have you ever heard the expression, 'Don't buck the system?' Well, in some cases, I say let's buck the crap out of it!

One system is what I started the book with: the way in which we are socially approaching masculinity and gender neutralizing. Another example of a system that we should buck is the belief that addiction is a disease, which is the prevailing *theory* in treating addiction, yet the system has the majority of us believing it to be *factual.* At Crossing the Jordan, we are vamping up a mission to expose that lie and demonstrate the truth about addiction instead. *We have successfully created an alternative approach that is producing a minimum of 8 times the success of other approaches to addiction.* It's time we buck this system and replace it with some common sense!

The reason I bring this up is because we women often get ourselves into trouble just accepting what we watch or read in the media as truth, allowing ourselves to be manipulated by a system that does not serve us, our family or our vision. We are often like sheep being led to the slaughter, unaware of the consequences of these imposed belief systems. We either settle for what they (the media and popular culture) dish out to us, out of ignorance, or we are too lazy to take a stand. Then one day we wake up to find our lives in a mess or unfulfilling.

Michael and I are 'disruptors'. Not out of pride or simple rebellion, but from refusing to blindly conform, preferring to 'disrupt' the status quo if it isn't serving people, and offering a viable alternative if possible instead. The people on our planet that take a stand are the change-makers and great leaders of our time. Far too often, we compromise out of ignorance or insecurity or just not wanting to deal with any pushback from those trapped in the 'system'. It takes courage to stand for something, especially when it's controversial. We tend to play it safe. More and more as I am in the public eye, I get blasted on social media for my beliefs on addiction, women's issues, masculinity, the fact that our residents earn their way through our programs, my criminal past, and my faith. It hurts. My team protects me when it gets brutal. However, I know what I stand for and choose to be unwavering.

When we decide to make a stand for *ourselves* and change our own lives, there is often a backlash as well. Transformation is radical. It makes the people in our lives uncomfortable because it reflects their belief systems back at them sometimes. Often your changes cause the people you love great discomfort because it impacts the family roles.

For instance, I was always labeled the black sheep in the family. So much so that I found myself embracing that identity…until it didn't serve me. Once I rejected that identity, officially changing, I didn't allow them to even joke about it with me anymore, and my family struggled with this. I was the one they needed to 'save.' Until I wasn't. My journey through suffering strengthened me, so when my mother passed away, and my family assumed I would run or fall apart, I was the one who ended up taking a stand, the one that held it together. My stand was that the rest of my life would be spent honoring my mother by becoming all that she desired me to be. I changed my role with my family and friends with this new attitude. They were very uncomfortable with the new version of me, and it was quickly clear that their comments and actions, (some of it subconsciously) were intended to put me back in their box. I refused to conform, and even 20 years later it is sometimes hard for them to let go of that earlier identification with me because it fed some unhealthy version of themselves. Only in recent years have they fully accepted the responsible, successful Dana, at almost 46 years old! I had to decide to keep my distance, with love, until they decided to honor me for the woman I became. When we decide to transform this often happens with the people closest to us. When you take a stand, be alert for people trying to push you over with their belief systems.

Another example of bucking the system is I live a fasted lifestyle. I don't eat at least 2 days a week and mostly only eat one meal a day when I do eat. The 'system' (the Standard American Diet which is SAD) tells us we must eat three meals or even several small meals a day. Science is proving that wrong. I have obviously lost a lot of weight since I began living this way and my health has dramatically improved, yet it's funny how upset and argumentative some people get with me, even with my success in this area staring them in the face. What's ironic is that they never said a thing when I was stuffing my face with sugar and carbs and had gained 40 pounds from emotional eating! My children skip meals and you'd think I was beating them from the reaction I get from some other parents! Why? Because I am disrupting the prevailing order or belief—and since it's *prevailing*—most people (sheeple) don't care to really seek answers for themselves or do their own research. (My children feel great by the way.)

It's important to note that I actually love following rules, ironically, because rules are designed to keep us safe. However, we must be wise about blindly following current trends without doing the work to research. We need to keep questioning what we 'know' to make sure it aligns with our vision for our lives or our values. I am not in any way inviting you to be a loud-mouthed rebel, though some of you *do* need to speak up and not be such a pushover. Some of us need to chill out and be more flexible and open. Taking a stand is *not* some overly-impulsive resistance to everything, that's immaturity. (We have plenty of that already going on). It's wise to follow rules. But if everyone's doing it, then it's wise to question *why*.

If you choose to do the work I've set out in this book, especially the *90-Day Challenge, the Sisterhood Quick Start Guide* or the *Be Hot Workbook*, your behaviors and beliefs will be revealed and challenged. When that happens, just examine them, ask yourself where the belief came from and if you truly believe or did you just conform out of fear or social pressure?

Do not conform to the pattern of this world but be transformed by the renewing of your mind.
- Romans 12:12

Be curious about the beliefs that you hold and why. Choose which ones are right, and take a stand, firmly. Be ready for any pushback and respond in humility, but don't you dare give in. If you get kicked onto your butt, get up, quickly. The world is counting on you to live excellently because you have a *purpose* and the world needs you. Be unique. Think for yourself. Never blindly conform. Being 'hot' and finding your man or enhancing your marriage is just a *part* of the plan for your life. Making an impact is what this life is about, and you can't do that all lonely, miserable and compromised.

It takes courage to take a stand. You are courageous or you wouldn't be reading this book right now! You're *ready* to make some changes. So, put your game face on, girl, you have a mission. The journey to self-possession has commenced. You are entering a new state of mind: poised, calm, confident and certain. Hold your head high and keep your shoulders back. Breathe in 'Today' and then exhale 'Yesterday', and all the 'days and years' before. Let it go. I'm beside you: *believing* the best in you and for you. Step fully into who you are meant to be—a woman of honor and courage—the rest will follow when you share your gifts and talents with the world.

Chapter 9

Service

Serving is sexy. The end. (I figured with all the serious personal growth stuff, it was time to have a little break and lighten up.) But really, service *is* sexy. The thing is we can't serve others to *become* sexy, but it does happen to make us extremely attractive as a bonus.

Michael just told me a story I totally forgot about. When we first met, there was this old bitter couple from his church, like they were old *and* mean, for real, but he loved them despite their crankiness and they had to move out of their house and needed help. He couldn't get *anyone* from church to help. Michael was so infuriated by that, and it kind of freaked me out a little because we had just started dating. I guess he was sick of the way people 'gave' their time, so he was passionately calling a few people out about it and in 'early Michael' style, he let em' have it. We both communicated so messily back then. We were led by our passions, and we often didn't express our emotions right. But I saw through to his heart motivation and it made mine flutter the way he was committed to serving, even a cranky elderly couple.

As I watched all this happening from the sidelines, the church members going back and forth, even close to fighting—my admiration for Michael grew. We were new together, so I didn't offer my opinion, I just quietly showed up at the house and started packing it up. Drama would occur around me during that day between people, but I just kept moving and packing and jumping in to lend a hand where needed, because I *loved* helping. I had longed to serve again, and I was excited to come alongside what Michael was so passionate about.

I had no idea that in the midst of all the chaos Michael was observing me closely. He told me only weeks ago when we were talking about this, that he would just look at me at different times throughout the day and his heart would just throb, watching me as I packed up the couple's treasures so carefully and was kind to everyone and genuinely serving his church family. He told me he began to fall in love with me that day, the Dana who quietly and cheerfully gave to others. The sweet thing is, throughout the day I was doing the same…watching him, his passion, the sweat pouring as he loaded the heavy appliances…and I watched him hug the cranky, ungrateful couple even though they badgered him all day to not drop anything. He would look at me and roll his eyes with the most adorable smile on his face. I wondered at him. He was so different than other men, in so many extraordinary ways. Our hearts to serve drew us close to one another, magnetically and magically.

The Gift of Service

I wish I understood the gift of service at a younger age. I don't dwell on regret, but I can't help but think about how different all our lives would look if we learned to die to *self* to truly *live*. The power of service can completely transform a life. I believe that serving our purpose together, living it out fully in our life, is the glue that holds it all together: marriage, parenting, our careers, our health and well-being in body, mind and spirit.

If we really understood the gift it brings I think our world would be a different place. Service takes humility and we could all use a little more of that. If we could just comprehend how powerful it is, to change things we desire to change in ourselves or in our lives, we would value service so much more. The mystery of denying serving ourselves ('dying' to our self) by serving others is we receive a greater blessing of freedom and joy from our act of giving. Most of us don't give selflessly very often. We operate mostly out of fear or selfishness. But when we do give, we get tenfold, hundredfold return...including much of what we desire as a person...once we stop thinking of ourselves and just start serving.

We live in a world of survival and disconnect, of self-indulgence and entitlement, with most never discovering the gift that service provides. I didn't. Not until I got to the end of myself. I mean, I remember loving the *feeling* when I did something for someone, but I didn't get the ripple effect it pays back into our whole lives, or outward, impacting others. We tend to isolate our times of service as a single event or act, but when we *embody* service and wrap our everyday lives around it is when we receive its greatest benefit.

It seems almost illogical to give up something without expecting anything in return, but this is a mystical principle of our universe. You will be given double for your trouble. We could play it safe and make service something we check off our list, if it even makes it into our lists at all. Or we could have faith and grace to make serving others a regular flow of love outwards from our lives.

Let's move mountains for ourselves by moving them for others.

The Purpose To Serve

When we are passionate about something, when have discovered our 'calling', when we know clearly what we are talented in or gifted with…this becomes our *purpose*. Service is the *action* of giving selflessly to fulfill that purpose. It flows naturally, effortlessly from the energy of our passion. And if we aren't *sure* of our purpose yet, we can still choose to serve an important cause we value. Our purpose *is* to *serve out of* our purpose. The only question now is *what is your special gift to the world?* Your contribution to mankind? And *how* will you serve the world with it? Our society functions because people serve, either through their actual jobs (if they're lucky) or through volunteering their time, energy, and talent in some other way.

Your purpose will dictate how you intend to serve others with the gifts you already know you have.

I'm a straight shooter, always have been. I'm creative and daring and I will take the risks most aren't willing to take. If you ask my childhood friends even today, they will tell you that they all saw that drive in me: to make the world a better place. I felt it inside, too. I could *feel* greatness inside me, aching to get out and accomplish what I was born to do. And then life happened. A series of bad choices and a trauma or two, and fear settled in to hold me back. Fear's entire job is to keep our purpose captured inside of us, never to be used for our unique contribution to the world.

If purpose wasn't so critical to mankind, we all wouldn't be longing to find our own. We talk about it all the time. Think about it: when someone has a crisis, depression or loss of some kind, all of us often end up discussing the sense that we are supposed to be doing something *more* with our lives. It's built into us to serve, to make a difference, to have an impact, to leave a legacy. When we connect with that calling, or gifting, is when everything begins to make sense.

In fact, *if we ever feel like our life is over, that maybe we've done the most unimaginable thing or had the worst of losses, we discover that the only way to peace, freedom and healing is through the gift of service.* Then there's what God does, takes something evil and uses it for good. Even experts agree that serving is good for the soul, healing our hearts and minds. Because of the gift of service, we *all* can have hope, and that it is *never* too late.

I can't tell you how many times Michael and I would be lying in bed and one of us will sit up suddenly, and say, "Oh my goodness, *that's* why I had to go through that! I was getting trained for *this.*" It's like every tear, every heartache, every failure can be turned around and used for good, interwoven somehow into our life of purpose to serve those that have lost hope. No, it's not a reason or excuse for the bad things in our lives, but it is a miraculous exchange that, out of darkness, light can result. That no matter what happens, our purpose still finds its way to us. Our purpose is our 'why' no matter where we are on the journey.

Your Purpose Doesn't Time Out

In our trainings, service is at the heart of all we do. Over the years though, I've discovered that some people have a problem receiving the benefits that come with serving out of their purpose. I see so many rob themselves of the abundant benefits because of their *attitude and perspective* towards service.

Our purpose, and the service required to live it out, does not have a completion date or a clock out time, because it's not meant to be an obligatory 'chore' to get over with, to move on to a more pleasant activity. Michael and I don't end our day thinking we've *'served our time'* towards our purpose in life, as if it's community service or a prison sentence. It never even crosses our minds, because what we do is our life and joy, and it just happens to be called 'service.' But I do see people thinking of it that way. They set boundaries and timelines on the amount of effort or time they are willing to serve their purpose. It just doesn't work like that, it's just not meant to be that way. If someone's punching in a timeclock with their service it probably means they haven't discerned what their purpose really *is*, because when we do, our entire lives—our time, our children, our marriage, and our careers—all interweave into our purpose, gladly. We embody our calling. It never ends, and you shouldn't want it to. Your purpose should set your soul on fire, where you can barely sleep and you can't wait to wake up, jump out of bed and start your day, in spite of how hard it could get, because you feel it in your veins that you are destined to do this *thing* that has *burning a hole inside of you* to get out and impact others! If you aren't living this way, this kind of life awaits you, it awaits all of humanity. Service is the greatest gift you could ever give *yourself* and all of those waiting to meet you.

> Don't ask yourself what the world needs. Ask yourself what makes you come alive and then do that. Because what the world needs is people who have come alive

-Howard Thurman

Service the Matchmaker

By default, when we think of where to find a man, we often think of a bar, pub or a nightclub. I don't know of all the places to meet singles, but traditionally for some reason that's the first place we think of. I think it's safe to say a bar is *not* the best place to find love. Online dating is the new meeting place norm in this busy world, and at least with online dating you can find out a little about the guy first, or get a sense of him a bit (if he has an honest bio).

I do have friends that got married after meeting in a bar so, yes, it can happen but it is rare that the marriage succeeds. Since it's so hard to find a good man these days anyways, why hurt our chances and shoot ourselves in the foot by meeting someone for the first time, while intoxicated, at a bar scene? If you are honestly happily married and you met in a bar, great! You beat the odds, so now let's just make it better!

I am about to share with you one of the single most important pieces of advice in this entire book, SO PAY ATTENTION:

Your greatest chances for success in finding a good man is at a service event, project or cause you get involved with and that you are passionate about. Period. (*Mic drop. Again.*)

Yes, this is your greatest chance of finding a good, compatible, passionate, honorable (even if still a little messy) man!

Now, here are my top three rules to identify and/or keep a good man:

Number One. Have integrity. You cannot fake being in your purpose, or quickly adopt one just to catch a guy. If you do, this lessens your chance of a successful connection with a good man through that purpose. Good men can smell compromise a mile away and it is NOT attractive, it reeks of desperation. Your purpose should ooze out of your pores, without having to tell him about it. It will telegraph out from the joy it brings you and he should see that authenticity in you. If you are unsure about your commitment to your current cause, don't stay unsure long, either get sure or move on. If you are putting conditions on or punching a timeclock with your purpose, that probably means you haven't really discovered it, either. You should be deep into what you are called to be, and he should be too, and then you meet in the midst of that. If he is not fully into his purpose but is committed, it may work. Basically, *be living and breathing your purpose, and not just for a few hours here and there.*

Number two. During the courting phase (and ever after that) you cannot abandon, compromise, give less time to or in any way *decrease your commitment to your purpose.* Not even for a first date. *Nothing.* You should be living joyfully in your purpose, your life entwined with all that it requires from you, including any sacrifices you will have to make or the time it will take from your social life. Basically, *don't give up on your purpose when you meet a guy.* Stay in integrity all through preparing, courting or dating, because fake won't make it.

Number Three. See if you can identify by how he lives his life, what *his* purpose is, and see how he responds to *yours.* Watch closely *how* he lives out his purpose, and what, if any, sacrifices he makes. This is the best indicator if he is a servant leader and it will be the best tool you have for getting rid of the selfish (unprepared) ones. If he isn't willing to support and serve alongside you after just meeting you, he won't ever. (Remember, we are on our best behavior at the beginning.) It takes humility to serve and a good humble man will lead, protect, and serve with you, without an agenda, in the power of agreement, to live out your purpose together as one unit, someday. *Walking powerfully in your purpose shouldn't intimidate a good man; instead he should be inspired by it and walk it with you.*

A woman's heart should be so hidden in God that a man has to seek Him just to find her.

- Maya Angelou

Not only should a good man have to find your heart, he should clearly understand his role in your purpose. His purpose may not be the same, but it shouldn't be in conflict with yours because *you* lead with what you love, and *you aren't willing to change who you are destined to be.*

If you are married and not walking in your purpose, the same exact rules apply. Discover and then dig into your purpose. Not selfishly, just passionately. Get buried in it. Serve. Give. Sacrifice. Don't require him to do it with you yet, until he sees how committed you are. Affirm him along the way. Let him know how amazing he is and pull out the long list of reasons you married him and compliment the daylights out of him as you continue to go after your purpose. It might get bumpy if you are doing something drastically different then you were before, but love will prevail in these situations.

If he is interested in what you are up to, great, share but don't get needy about it and for the love of God, don't expect an award from your husband for your courage to go after your purpose. That's not attractive and it makes it less about giving and all about you. Instead, focus outwardly on the beneficiaries of your gift of service, and in time, the rest will fall into place.

Michael and I have successfully counseled at least six married couples in recent years that have wonderful marriages today because this is what they focus on: *serving together.* The married couples understand when their husband or wife can't be home because they are giving to others. Each of them cheers the other on. Having a purpose together also breathes new life into the marriage over and over again if you keep serving.

Yes, a good woman should discover what her purpose is *before* she finds a good man, but I don't mean that you have to have it *all* figured out. But eventually you must be aware of what you are gifted in, be actively pursuing that purpose, and leading your life with a servant's heart. If you are not proficient in this when you meet a good man, your purpose will take a backseat, and your marriage will begin to wither and be unfulfilling—because you will have compromised yourself for the sake of him or your own selfish desires, which never works and always leads to a kind of spiritual death.

We must be on mission for a cause greater than ourselves. The entry level mission is to serve your family and friends, then it progresses to society and then on to humanity, or mankind. The bigger the mission, the better the chance of living an abundant life and not falling back into our old problems. So, serve *big*. Set aside your own needs for a while and watch how the abundance flows. It's miraculous how it all works; a supernatural exchange that flows beyond what we can fully comprehend. The real test of our maturity is to serve someone who could never repay us— that is when we know we have ultimately 'arrived'.

There are these lyrics that Nichole Nordeman sings:

I want to leave a legacy,

How will they remember me?

Did I choose to love?

Did I point to you enough?

To make a mark on things

I remember when I heard these words the first time, they penetrated me and shook me out of my selfish thoughts. I had relapsed after eight years clean and sober, and shame consumed me. I was driving, it was a breezy warm autumn day. I rolled down the window and smelled the fresh air and looked up into the sky, with tears rolling down my cheeks. It hit me that I had forgotten my mission and had gotten sucked back into my old ways. I believe it happened because my mission had shrunk. Where I had once served big, making my problems seem small, the current smallness of my contribution made my problems seem big. You see, the bigger our service, the smaller our problems.

I had once sung these lyrics before when I had been serving other women in prison, so when I heard the song on the radio, a flood of memories washed over me, taking me back to a much happier time when I was in prison, (weird, huh?) serving others. I had been released from the prison cells but because my contribution had gotten smaller and smaller, my problems had gotten bigger and bigger. Freedom is never free. Sacrifice and service is where freedom lives.

That was the last day I ever relapsed, many years ago. I sang those words at the top of my lungs and I decided to leave a legacy. I decided that I will fill a stadium with people on the day of my funeral. Yes, I will pack a stadium filled with people I impacted for good. I am *that* committed to make a mark on things, so that you remember me because I chose to love. Just as the lyrics inspired, I am that committed to serving. It's scary to share that vision with you right now but the more vulnerable I make myself about this, the more likely I am to fulfill that dream. Since everything I have envisioned has come to pass so far, I will take a stand for this maximum impact and spend the rest of my days going about doing good. Who knows, maybe you will be there at the stadium, at my funeral. If I'm going to dream of touching lives why not dream big? Service is the key that opens the door to greatness. Treasure the gift of service. It will always serve *you*.

The people who are crazy enough to think they can change the world are the ones who do.

— Steve Jobs

Are you crazy enough to think you can change the world? I am. Why can't you, too? Go for it. Get busy figuring out your purpose out, if you haven't already. Serve at local events, fitness expos, triathlons and marathons, writing conferences, disaster relief, animal shelters, youth groups, mission trips, senior living—whatever it is you're passionate about. Don't limit yourself to a soup kitchen. (That's the first way to serve that comes to mind but there is more, so much so.) Give art lessons, drive at-risk kids to concerts, clean up beaches, serve on a medical ship in another country—anything you love but just start serving—because if you don't know your purpose yet, it will help you discover it the fastest.

A good man will find you because you are self-possessed woman, with a sisterhood and a purpose you love. Let your purpose be your matchmaker. Let your love for others be what draws him to you. It's the secret sauce to the kind of love that lasts forever.

Chapter 10

Sex

Sex. It's a tough subject, especially in our modern feminist culture. The conversation around sex and feminism tends towards boasting about liberation and freedom, to wear whatever, act however, and sleep with as many partners as we choose. Which, its true we have that freedom, but at what cost?

So, let me start with my story. I have had many sexual seasons of my life during my 46 years on earth. I have swung towards both ends of the pendulum——from promiscuous to prudish. You are probably talking to one of the few women that has empathy towards all spectrums to the degree that I do because of the crazy life I led. It's tough to admit my promiscuity: I've been to strip joints, sex clubs (sorry, Dad) and I have lied to myself about how wonderful it feels to do whatever I want. Well, I learned there is *nothing* liberating about being promiscuous, unless you are deceiving yourself, have become desensitized or have allowed your emotions to atrophy. (I can just hear the screams from the feminists right now.) Hold on to your liberated panties!

I was also a total religious nut job for a minute, desperate to get women to understand the dangers of sleeping around. I almost lost my relationship with my oldest daughter because I was so hard on her. Pushing your views on anyone backfires.

There is a path to freedom, but it's not paved with one-night stands, or being too afraid to admit you wanted more than sex from a guy while acting like you didn't. Oh, there are many women that live this way, no doubt. I've met them, I've heard their arguments, I've watched as they pretended it didn't hurt. I've seen the look of pain in her eyes beneath the expression of disdain when a woman glares at me like I'm some outdated conservative whacko. *Save it.* I am anything but that, so, sorry girl, I clearly see the *loneliness* on your face when he doesn't call you back, and I can hear the pain in your voice when you've *compromised,* yet again.

I've walked hundreds of women through the transformation process. I've worked intimately with many prostitutes that come to me claiming "It's no big deal, it's just a job, and it's *my* body". That is until they cry in my arms for hours, confessing the pain of rejection and regret. I've spent so many group sessions with women that start the meetings by saying that sex before marriage is no big deal, but when given the opportunity to confess their truth in a safe place, they share that they wish they had waited for the right man that would love them forever.

It's just crap. All of it. We *want* to wait, we just live in a culture that has made waiting uncool or worse...*forgotten.*

I hereby boldly and courageously proclaim to you that I intend to make *'waiting to have sex'* cool again!

There, I said it. All problems solved! Womankind is now restored and *truly* liberated to wait for the man that will treasure, honor, respect, provide and protect her, till death does he part.

Hang in there with me, now, because I am so, so serious about this. I know I am at risk of losing you right now but sister, we've come this far together so just hang with me for a few more chapters. *I will not judge you, whatever your stance is.* I imagine many of you are living with your boyfriends right now, so I have some stories to tell you because I did the same. I'm just holding you to your commitment to stay with me and be open until the end of the book. If at the end you still don't like my advice, you can go back to your life and your relationships as they are.

You Know You Want To

I realize that I am talking 'crazy' right now. I lost my virginity at 16. It was not cool how it went down and in no way did it even come close to how I had imagined it would be. Many of us have had the same experience.

At that point, it changed the vision of what I thought sex and my future was going to look like. I realized and accepted that my sex life wouldn't fit the picture I had dreamed of, and it seemed to open this door of nihilism that I had no idea how to close, and I wasn't sure if I really wanted to close it, and I certainly didn't know the emotional toll it would take on my life. I just started to have sex with men, period. By promiscuous I mean I slept with men, not a crazy amount of them, just enough to find a man that *wanted* me, that wanted to *be* with me, beyond the bedroom.

Can you relate? I think you can.

I think we are too afraid to admit that we wish we *hadn't* had sex before marriage, as if we will be judged by others or worse, judge ourselves, thus forcing ourselves to face any regret or pain we've buried inside over it. The thing is, we already do beat ourselves up about it, unknowingly. It comes out in self-destruction: depression, loneliness, addiction, isolation or even suicide. Yes, I am connecting casual sex with suicide. Many women hurt so deeply from the pain of rejection that they die, either by killing themselves quickly or slowly—it's the fricken' truth. I'll be brave enough to speak the truth and not put 'icing on shit', as I like to say.

I'm not trying to make sex bad, judge you, or even convince you that casual sex is wrong. I am not putting anyone in a box, labeling them, making a religious point or trying to hurt you or shame you about casual sex. That's not my point! I've been there and done all of it, too! I *am*, however, bringing into the light, that as women we feel yucky, hurt, rejected, alone, unworthy, and, might I say, *unclean* if we give ourselves freely sexually to someone in the heat of the moment only to discover afterwards they want nothing *more* than sex. It just isn't good for *us*. It is painful and destructive, more than we like to admit to ourselves, much less out loud…and certainly way more painful than any feminists will ever admit.

The mountain of media messages we get from the radical feminists, the magazines, the steamy novels, all say that a woman has a right to do whatever she wants with her body. Of course we have that right! Hey, I'll scream that from the mountaintops with you! But the freedom to choose means accepting the consequences of our choices, of our actions. Just because we are 'free' to do something doesn't automatically mean it's beneficial for us.

So, how about we keep 'waiting to have sex' in the conversation, respectfully? Let's not swing so far the other way and make 'waiting' some kind of weakness, either. On the contrary, we are badass women if we have the self-discipline to wait, and make a man wait, too. Now, that can be super-hot.

Second Chances

I remember the day I decided I was going to wait on sex till I got married. I was sitting in my prison cell, pleading with God to renew my soul, to heal my heart, and give my mind a 'clean slate' again. Yes, that was my specific request. I just wanted to feel fresh and whole again, with the stain of my past washed away. He did what I asked, and I remember the moment I felt restored and newly alive. At *that* new moment, I committed to stay whole, to guard this new me by not ever giving myself away to anyone but a good man I chose to marry.

But then I got out of prison, and was feeling sexy, fit, ready for a new life, and temptation hit. No, I didn't sleep around but I broke that promise to myself. I put myself in a few tempting situations and ended up giving in to an old friend, then justified it to myself. Then, I justified it one more time...and then one more time...and then the third and last time, with Michael.

Michael and I moved in together very quickly. I was madly in love and it certainly was not about sex, but my broken promise was there, in the back of my mind, not as a condemning thought this time, but as an invitation to myself of freedom...from com-

promising myself anymore in any way, by just deciding to WAIT. I remembered *why* I committed to myself to wait for the right man: I knew a *good man* would honor this request, and this was the clearest and quickest way to test who a man really is and not waste any more time on losers. It didn't matter that the world was giving me permission to have sex freely, I refused to listen because I had a vision and I was not going to allow lies to steal it from me this time.

Michael got a DUI and went to jail. It seemed our lives were in danger of going in the wrong direction. We confessed some of our wrongs to each other on the phone as he sat in the waiting area, and then—almost simultaneously—we both blurted out, "I don't want to have sex again until we are married." Until that moment, neither of us knew the other had felt this way but both of us knew we wanted more than what we were giving ourselves to. There'd been a few brief comments about waiting, but since we had already had sex it seemed pointless, until that moment when we were both brave enough to speak our truth.

That moment shifted us in a direction I am in awe of every day of our lives. When Michael got home, we openly shared our commitment with our family and friends, asking them to hold us accountable (even though most of them thought we were crazy), and we waited the eight months until we married.

Once, during that time, while we laid on the grass in the park, I straddled Michael, teasing him. He lifted me off him firmly, looked me in the eye and said, "Don't ever tempt me like that again. I will honor you until the day we marry." I could have fainted right there in the park. My former-bad-boy-now-good-man-soon-to-be-future-husband just honored me in a way that is only dreamed about in fairy tales. He smiled at me after setting me next to him on the grass, kissed me on the cheek and said, "You are *that* worth it."

Over those eight months of waiting, we really got to know each other, and it created this unbreakable bond between us. Honestly I struggled to wait more than he did. Michael said because he had waited for me so long, and knowing I had arrived, it was easy to wait only a little longer.

On our wedding day, I kept waiting for this *Moment,* when I would connect with the reality of all that had happened to get to this day, that my prayers had been answered, that the man I had waited for had honored me and decided to *wait* for me. I remember walking towards my father, sad that I didn't feel the way I thought I would feel. I looked at my dad, nervous, anxious as he reached out to put my hand into his arm to walk me down the aisle.

And then, *it happened.* I felt the Moment, the connection of it all, and the weight of awe settled on me right as the doors flew open and I heard the wedding song begin, and I looked into my father's eyes and he smiled and said, "You did it, baby. Yes, this is really happening. And yes, it was worth the wait."

At the end of the aisle, Michael was there: handsome, smiling, waiting…with eyes glistening. He looked at me and gave his standard wink and nod. *I was worth it,* he was saying, in his own special sign language. His eyes were telling me that all I had done in the past didn't matter—my foolishness, my insecurities, my heartache. It was over, and now I was his. He would protect me and lead me, and he was mine and we had overcome it all, together.

Let's Be Honest

If that story sounds corny, I don't care. It's 100% true. Be honest, at least half of you love the story and wouldn't mind your own version of it. The other half of you are *convinced* that you need to 'try a man on for size' before you marry him.

The thing is, although Michael and I had sex before marriage, I would have loved it if we hadn't. I had tried enough men on for size and it just doesn't matter in the long run. Let's talk about the whole 'trying it on first' maxim: so if he isn't good in bed but is of extraordinary character, would you really 'pass' on him because of the sex alone? Um, no. (Yeah, a few of you are saying yes. But only a few of you!) If a man exhibits all the qualities you want in a good man, are you really not going to marry him because of the way he is, or isn't, in bed? I call bull crap if you say yes, especially with the shortage of good men these days.

Yes, sex matters. Yes, if he is good in bed, it's a big win. But good sex is a progressive thing in marriage, it gets better with practice and communication, because a good man will learn and listen and please you how you want to be pleased. Even sex is a character issue, not a sexual one. But, I get it. I have had some horrible lovers, too, most of us have. The truth is they were probably horrible in other areas, which spilled over into the sex. Maybe they were sloppy or unhealthy or lazy or selfish and all that shows up in the bedroom. Get a good man, and he will work with you to get it right in the bedroom, because it starts in his heart, not his pants.

Sarah and I have been hearing this new conversation going on, especially among married women executives. This new (or maybe very old) trend women are doing with men: raising their children with their husband, then getting a lover and divorcing their husband. Oh my, have the tables turned. These women are claiming empowerment. That's not empowerment, it's entitlement, and it leads to destruction. How is it in any way less destructive than when men have done it? It may be fun in the short term, or maybe even exciting and wild for a long time, but it sure the hell isn't honorable.

If you do this, most likely you are only replacing your husband with an unqualified or unprepared man because a good man won't hop in the sack with a woman who behaves this way. You'll find men like this to sleep with, for sure. They might even be younger and hotter, but they are not good men...and eventually *you* will be replaced. No judgement, you can have at it. Tell yourself whatever you please, but I'd sure like us to chat in five years after that mess.

Sisters let's at least be honest about our way of being. Frankly, I don't think this type of woman would have read past the first three chapters, so they are likely long gone. Let's be aware of the chatter among us. Look, its ok whatever way you think, I will not put anyone in a box and Lord knows, I will stick it out with you no matter what, but let's admit we have quite a mess on our hands. We have an endless stream of garbage being poured in between our ears and we are calling all kind of things 'noble': liberty, sexual freedom, empowerment, a woman's choice, blah, blah, blah, blah. I've tried all this crap on for size and it leads to one thing—emptiness. Worse, this is the message our daughters are getting.

You are free to believe whatever you want, *free* to believe a lie if you so choose, but if you took a poll, if women could do a big do-over, they would go back to that little girl who still wants to live happily-ever-after. And before you disregard my opinion, re-member: *I coach and train women from every background and I have been around more blocks than most.* I've heard it all and I've done most of it and at the end of the day, women hunger for good, honorable men that are willing to wait for them.

I am going to fight like hell to make 'waiting to have sex' cool again. Do you have any idea of the kind of self-control that's required by a man to honor a woman this way? Do you get the restraint and character needed to wait for sex? It takes one hell of a good man. Michael didn't like how he felt by dishonoring me and he made it right, almost immediately. Michael gets hit on all the time, but through discipline and honor he became (and stays) a good man. We could sure use a little more of those.

So…we agree it hurts to give your body away and not be hon-ored the way you always hoped you would be, the way you *deserve* to be. We've all cried our share of tears from the loss of what we had hoped for. Waiting for sex in the relationship allows for the discovery phase to run its course and it is the fastest, most reli-able strategy you have in getting rid of the bad, unprepared men. Use it as a tool to weed out the weeds. Give yourself a chance. If the single biggest decision of your life is who your life mate will be, why not take it very seriously?

It's sensible to withhold sex so you can expedite the process and not waste your time with losers. If we are so advanced in our thinking, why is it so hard to consider that waiting is a good game plan, an intelligent course of action to find love and live in abun-dance? I'm all for being strategic!

Driven to Have Sex

Men have a sex drive. Biology *drives* them to want to have sex. They are responsible for their behavior, of course, but the desire to have sex, and the temptation to do so, is a constant reality for them. For my married sisters, we had better not ignore this truth. On one hand, we have women showing off their bodies more every day and on the other hand (and at the same time), we have married women 'letting themselves go'. It's a recipe for disaster. It shouldn't be *so* shocking if a husband succumbs momentarily to temptation. I am not letting men off the hook, not for a minute, and I am certainly not asking married women to let it 'all hang out' either, but it is important to be aware of the reality and not dismiss or ignore it. A good man will navigate successfully through these rough waters but let's help him out and keep the spice in the marriage.

Married women often expect what they didn't require in the beginning of their dating. We put a ton of expectation on our husband's behavior, in bed or otherwise, that we didn't set up for his success at the beginning. If you were having sex all the time at the beginning and suddenly start withholding based on how you feel about yourself, it's a set up for a man that had you at his pleasure and then is suddenly cut off. (I'm sorry, I am going to really stir things up here, but it is your responsibility as his wife to be available to him, as it is his, to be available to you). Some of us women are more sexual than our husbands. Either way, if you don't pay attention to sex, the ever-present lustful pressure out there will run havoc on your marriage. When we withhold sex and don't communicate why, we run the risk of an extramarital event occurring. It's as if we keep a crack in our bedroom door for a mistress to walk right in. Of course, I'm not suggesting you be mistreated, or his sex slave, but *wake up*…it's a plausible *reality*.

So, keep it hot and spicy and fun. Be confident in who you are and be vulnerable with him. That potential mistress is always out there, waiting on the other side of your bedroom door. You have all the power to keep her out and keep your husband interested in you. Remember, he chose to marry *you*. So, light some candles occasionally, whisper sweet nothings in his ear and have fun having sex with your husband.

A Fine Line

I believe we need to leave a little mystery while embracing our femininity. We can be sexy *AND* classy in our appearance and our behavior. I work hard every day at presenting myself in a way that makes my husband still hot for me but doesn't trip up other men and tempt them. It's a balance, a fine line and a self-possessed woman can walk it beautifully. It's our job to learn how to hold ourselves in a way that is both sexy and still honoring to ourselves and the man we love (or hope to love in the future.)

I see so many women wade in dangerous waters with regards to this balance, here. They don't see the difference between staying sexy for their husband and flirting with/tempting other men. Sometimes women have changed their body or behaviors for their husbands and when he doesn't notice quick enough, she will seek attention from other men. That's not honorable. Make the change in you for other reasons, not just to get your man or entice your husband. We really need an inner transformation to be an excellent human on the outside, then the change will last. If we are doing it solely for our husbands' attention, we can get hurt if he doesn't respond quickly enough. If you want sex and he doesn't, that can feel like rejection. Just keep being the newest and best version of you and he will eventually notice because you will be living in the kind of confidence that turns his head. Give it time. We don't get ourselves in unhappy situations overnight and neither will spicing up the sex life. Don't give up and don't give in to hurt. Just be patient and keep your eyes on your husband and no one else. *He'll notice.*

If you are single, don't behave as if you are casting a net for anyone that is available. Stay classy and poised as if you aren't available to just anyone. Hold your intimate space in a way that let's men know they must work at it, that you are reserving yourself for the good man you've been waiting for. Hold the line. Good men notice the way good women hold themselves and will be drawn naturally to that excellence.

Be French

French women are notoriously known for how they keep the love alive in marriage.

Jo Piazza, the author of *'What I Learned From Real Women on Five Continents About Surviving My First Really Hard Year of Marriage'* writes: "We aren't set up for success here," Piazza shares of women in the United States. "Too many of us move far away from our families, communities, and support system, which puts an awful lot of pressure on a spouse to be one person's absolute everything."

Piazza continues "American women think that they need a man to fulfill them," one French woman explains. "We [French women] fulfill ourselves and then we find a man to come along and be part of our journey." Not only do the French maintain independence within relationships, they insist on making sure their partner knows they are confident with themselves. "None of the whining 'Ooohhhhh I look fat in this dress...I look old!' He will believe what you tell him to believe about you. You tell him you feel beautiful and thin and young and sexy and that is what he will think of you." Put more simply: "The more you love yourself, the more your husband will love you."

The writer explains, "It's work for him. He still needs to 'conquer me' every day and I need to make him want me every day. I need to put in the effort—and here's what's important: I *want* to do the work," Piazza's friend says. As another friend puts it: "No one wants to be cheated on. No one wants to see their man with another woman...You behave like his mistress and it is less likely to happen." The trick, many French say, is to stay mysterious. "Stop peeing with the door open. Keep some things private!"

We have become vulgar and crude as American women and further, we are entitled about our way of being. Not *every* woman, no, but there is a common *tone*...so much so that our fellow sisters across the oceans know it about us. Our 'anything goes' attitude has stripped us of some of the beauty of our femininity, the elegance of who we are. We have become sloppy in so many ways: sexually, sensually, physically...as we cheer one another on in our 'right' to be loud, bossy, unrefined and obscene. Indeed, you have a right to be whomever you choose but who do you really *want* to be? *How* do you want to be perceived? What are the *results* that you truly desire?

When we are alone in our bedrooms, craving the respect and love of a good man or the husband we love, I believe that the noise about our 'rights' goes quiet and we are left longing to be a woman of elegance and grace, respected among honorable men and women. Let the noise of the world go silent and ask yourself: how do I present myself sexually to the world? When you close your eyes, take a breath, and picture your body in your minds' eye, do you look alive and sensual, honorable and respected?

Poupie Cadolle, the CEO of one of France's oldest lingerie companies, explains to Piazza. "For a French woman, a beautiful set of underwear is part of her personality. She does not save it for a special occasion. She wears it because she wants to feel beautiful every day. American women wear underwear like a uniform." Piazza continues, 'And though many may find the following advice old-fashioned or anti-feminist, Cadolle also says that a woman should let her man pick her lingerie. "American women do not understand this. They would never bring their husbands with them into the shop and ask them what they like. In France we care what our husband likes. We have a confident relationship with what our husband likes. We let him come and see and choose. And then…we let him pay. French husbands always pay."

The French put great effort into seducing their husbands and keeping the romance alive. Piazza shares what a French wife says, "When you go out to dinner put down your damn phone and don't talk about work or the laundry or the broken toilet. Would a man talk about a broken toilet with his mistress?" one French woman says. "Speak about things that are interesting, and leave the nagging to his coworkers," another recommends. "Don't pick small fights; don't speak of small things. And above else, never be boring."

Let's make our men miss us sometimes. If Michael is out of town or busy in the evening, I let him be gone so that he craves to come home to me. Michael says he can barely stand to cross over the Golden Gate Bridge because he longs for me when he crosses over. He'll even call me and tell me so. I *let* him long for me. I am intentional about how Michael perceives me, and I am quite clear when I desire to be chased, sexually. I tell him I *want* him, but never that I am needy for him. I don't pee in front of Michael, but I make sure he sees my body in the light when I step out of the shower. It wasn't always this way; I trained myself to be brave and sexy *for* him, and for him alone. He sees the men look at me and he notices that I see them watching yet I keep my eyes on him. When I feel sexy and alive, I make sure Michael notices that I only have eyes for him, and he does the same for me. I know it takes effort to keep the romance alive and it is my honor to make him want me, in every possible way. I can get Michael to do anything I want because of the woman I choose to be *for* him. He just wants to do what I want because I honor his needs and I treasure his desires. Because I intend to *keep* my man and never let a mistress into my bedroom.

The French understand clearly that happy and healthy relationships require a lot of work. French women tend to understand their responsibility, especially in the areas of seduction and sex.

To my American sisters: be like the French! Be the woman that walks into a room and everyone notices. *Wait* for a good man so you *know* he is good, and then seduce your husband for the rest of your life. We all want to *be* that woman, and we can. It's who we are meant to be…Sensual. Feminine. *Alive.*

Chapter 11

Your Vision

> ## Where there is no vision, there is no hope.
> ### - George Washington Carver

Because of the internet and today's social media culture, we are exposed now more than ever to invitations and opportunities for personal development and to create a vision for ourselves. Inspiring posts telling us to pursue our dreams and remind of us of *who we want to be* or *what we want to do* someday. Yet some statistics state that only 2% of the population accomplish their life goals or live out the vision they have for their life. With the ever-present threat of information overload via the internet it is more tempting that ever to just 'fulfill our dreams' virtually by watching others live them out on our screens. Additionally, what is meant for inspiration can easily turn in to comparing, which discourages or even paralyzes our own process of moving our aspirations into reality.

There is risk, fear, and a cost to make it all 'real'…and these costs and limitations worm their way into our psyches until one day we wake up and find that we have become the 98% of those that never fulfill our dreams. *So how do we become the 2% that do?*

Your Vision

The first step is to discover what your vision *is*. Many of us know already, but others can spend a lifetime wondering (or telling themselves they don't know so they don't have to be responsible for their contribution to the world). I propose that *you know quite well* what your vision is for your life: maybe not the full version of the story, but you know some first steps, a direction, at least *one* desire living inside of you, to start with.

Maybe you have a picture in your heart, that's tangible enough you can touch it at times. It's there in your thoughts, in your minds eye, and you recognize it but maybe you've thought it was too lofty of a vision for *you*, or too big of a dream from where you are *now*. A lack of faith may be stopping your from executing that vision. Fear may be terrifying you out of believing in your vision at all. Or maybe you've buried your dreams so deep for so long that you can't connect to it at all.

Whatever it is…WAKE IT UP. Your vision has a purpose, it's needed in our world. Your dreams are *never* too big. As long as you are breathing there is time, energy and resources to make your vision a reality. It's never too late, you are never too old, you are always enough, and these days you have the training available at your fingertips to execute all of it. Take it one step at a time.

So, how do we bring our dreams to life again? We have to connect to them *emotionally*. Emotion is what drives the vehicle (your body) to get to where you want to go (your vision). The emotional connection to your vision is there somewhere, buried deep or maybe it is starting to bubble up to the surface, but it will be recognizable as tingling, terrifying, or exhilarating when you think of it. When you allow yourself to imagine the possibility that it could really happen, that there is much more available for you, the excitement begins to wash over you. Either way, you *already have what it takes inside of you*…so, connect with it. Breathe that vision back to life or fan the flame you already have burning but CONNECT, to your vision, to your dream, what you believe you have been called to do, to be, to give to generously towards, so that your life *means* something and you have a purpose, a difference to make in the world for good.

You don't have to have it all figured out right away. When I was given the vision for Crossing the Jordan, it didn't look fully like it does now. I envisioned a home for women and children with a social enterprise for funding the home. But now? Oh, my Lord! *God is using that vision to turn our society's approach to addiction completely upside down!* Yes, I'll be that bold. *We are currently experiencing a minimum of 8 times more success than the national average for recovery from addiction.* EIGHT TIMES!

Our entire organization (way beyond my own vision now) feels called to bust out the theory or prevailing axiom that 'addiction is a disease'. I believe someday soon we will be invited to the White House to discuss a better way to deal with the opiate crisis we have in our country. *Talk about dreaming big!* You wanna know how I can be so bold to write down this vision so clearly to you now? Because I have stepped out in faith and spoken boldly about the purpose I have been called to fulfill so many times that I have developed the kind of faith that moves mountains. I am unafraid to put my visions out there because we *become* what we believe, and we manifest what we speak out loud. Our thoughts and words hold creative power. I know who I am, whether you believe what I say or not. I don't need people's approval because I am not afraid to fail. I have learned that if my vision doesn't manifest in a way that I imagined it to be, it's a good thing: it likely isn't the right time, I need to shift my perspective or I need to right a wrong somewhere. *Then*, it will come to pass. It always has, and I believe it always will. Our possibilities are limitless.

Let me be clear, though, I didn't start like this, I wasn't always this brave. Those early days were scary, and I did it all *afraid*. Yes, I've always believed I would be instrumental in creating a massive change. I did. Really. I knew, right in the midst of misery and self-doubt, I knew someday I would do something great, for women, for the world. I just didn't know how to move through it and see past my current reality. I had created the biggest mess of my life. The passion I felt inside never seemed big enough to counter the reality of my circumstances. Why? *Because I didn't understand the purpose of my defeat.* No, there is no excuse for what I did wrong and I take full responsibility. Yet I don't think we will ever fully comprehend how all our misfortunes work together for our good, here on earth. How our pain can help others gain.

It's beyond my comprehension, so I just choose to believe the best and use my mistakes to gain wisdom.

Your failures will shape you, strengthen you, build you with reserves to withstand the hard times. Living out your vision will be hard but so what? Life is hard anyway. Our vision is what inspires us to *keep going* through it, making the hard times worth it, giving it meaning and a purpose for it all!

I look back on my 5 years in that prison cell and I am *grateful*. I am thankful for my incarceration because, in my suffering, I found freedom. I discovered my purpose in the middle of my pain. There isn't a day that passes that I don't use the tools I learned through the process of that epic failing. I use those tools to guide others through their pain so I do not regret one day in that lonely cell. I intentionally approached my experience locked away as training like in *The Karate Kid*. I live out my vision today on the skills I got behind bars. I am a warrior because I trained well and I stay fit for life so I may encourage others to find meaning in their misery. We use the broken road to find our way home.

However, we don't *have to* understand all the whys, and shaking our fist at God and complaining about yesterday never serves us for our future. We may never comprehend the fullness of our vision and its purpose until we leave this planet. Life tends to give us our instructions in doses, as we become more prepared and equipped with each mission. Keep your eyes on the mission, not the position.

I could not have handled the magnitude of my purpose on earth if God had showed me how big my vision would end up being. The weight of it would have crippled me. Fear of failure or even selfishness would have paralyzed me if I knew in advance the hard work it would take to see this vision to its fruition. That's why we are given doses based on what we can handle. *I did, however, understand that I had a choice to say yes or no to my purpose, a choice to accept who I was called to be and then a choice to joyfully begin to walk in the right direction.* That is all it takes. It doesn't have to be complicated or overwhelming. *You choose to say yes then when you walk in those gifts and talents over time it becomes natural to do it with ease.* When you fall in step with who you were born to be, as tough as the battle can be at times, doors that once were shut just miraculously open, people who would never believe in you have their eyes opened, and the gates to the freedom you are longing to experience swing open.

Pain is the Greatest Trainer

I often train others to walk out their vision and I love to use *The Karate Kid* metaphor with them. The Karate Kid was painting the fence, washing the car, sanding the floors, never understanding at the time that he was being trained and equipped to fight and *win.* Our failures in life are like those chores his sensei was training him with: you feel worn out, sore, tense, you are frustrated because the training doesn't make sense and seems like a waste of time, it's hard and you just want to give up. Then, oh, THEN one day you find yourself up against real adversity, some force trying to stop you from fulfilling your dream and all of a sudden you remember your training instinctively, you face down that adversity—and you kick its ass. You automatically respond to the temptation to quit in a *new* way, and you win by pushing you're your previous limitations. Now you are strong, brave and you face your fears because you have trained well. All your failures, pain and suffering are suddenly used for good. You have overcome your circumstances, allowing you to authentically connect with others with empathy, and you can now *train them* for their vision. Now your failures can help, not just yourself, but others, expanding the potential for good.

Do not accept where you are as your final destination. Do not let your life be ruled by randomness. Choose. Write down whatever is stirring around inside of you right now as you read my words. Don't worry if it isn't perfectly planned out, just take the first step with *faith*. Faith is believing in what you cannot see, *yet*. Be bold and expect that as you take each step, the light will shine beneath your feet and your path will be made clear.

Deep down you *know* your heart's desire, you know what you are hungry for. You weren't made to be insignificant, you were made on purpose, for a purpose. Your vision gives you the reason to get out of bed. Set your soul on fire and go for it.

Don't Look Back

Don't look back, I said, *you're not going that way any way*. It doesn't matter where you are, where you've been, the wrongs you've done, the behaviors you have, your current beliefs, your family dynamics, how much money you have or don't have—not one damn bit of it makes a difference in becoming the best version of you *today*.

'Every day is a new day.' I know it sounds trite, or it sounds cool for a moment and then, ouch, reality hits us in the face, but it IS true. Tomorrow will be a *new* day that will make today *yesterday* when you wake up in the morning. You must simply *decide to not let yesterday define you*.

The truth is yesterday is *gone*; it's in the rearview mirror. Keep it there. I look back occasionally only to see how far I've come, to enjoy the view, or to check if my blind spots are clear, but not out of regret. I can look back and celebrate the milestones with gratefulness but I don't focus on where I left. Where I left was yesterday. I stay focused on today and excited about tomorrow.

Most people allow who they are or who they were to hold them back. The story we tell ourselves about our life will either hold us back or propel us forward. When we allow unforgiveness, regret or self-pity to consume us, we are stuck in yesterday, to stay.

When we deny our story, it defines us. When we own the story, we can write a brave new ending.

- Brene Brown

Listen, *you get to write the brave new ending!* I remember the very day I decided to write mine. It seemed so simple by the time I got to that point. Why in the hell was I letting who I *was* stop me from being who I knew I was called to be? You know what it was? *People.* I was letting the opinion of others keep me stuck in the past. That's what losers do and I wasn't a loser, anymore. I refuse to be average or mediocre so why would I ever let others hold me back? My children loved me no matter what and my husband was right by my side. *So why would I let strangers ever keep me down?*

Do not be incarcerated by how others define you.

It's *insane* the power we give to people we don't even know, or if we do, don't respect. If they loved us, they wouldn't hold us back in the first place. Listen, *people won't like it when you leave them behind in their misery.* So, what? Let them go. Attach yourself to winners. Invest in you! Don't hurt people while pursuing your dreams but focus on where you are headed and don't let *anyone* tear you down. Add value to others on *their* journey, as well. Remember, you need a tribe of solid sisters.

Remember, this is *your* vision, for *your* life. As you step out into it, the critics will reveal themselves. Don't be bitter with them, just be grateful that you are not incarcerated by their definition of you. Release them in love. Be careful to not declare your vision from a negative place, like out of revenge or with anger in your voice, or that you are going to 'do it your way.' That's not how a God-given purpose is developed.

Simply walk calmly and kindly away from those people in your life. As you do, there will be those that try to pull you backwards, but with grace and honor, free yourself from their tugging. They can't linger in your life for long if you don't let them.

Believe in who you are and find others who will too, and you will eventually build a team of winners to cheer you on.

Whatever It Takes

I think you can tell by now, I'm an all-or-nothing kind of girl. I really do consider myself quite the badass. Michael reminds me that we are not *all* called to be 'warrior women' so he cautions me not to assume you, dear reader, can handle my direct calls to action. Wrong again, Michael (respectfully so)! *You're a man, designed to protect me,* I think to myself, *I say all women are warriors!*

Michael, of course, has a point…to a degree. He *is* right that we are not *all* called to go into *heavy battle* the way in which I am called to do, for example. I am in direct contact with sex traffickers, pimps, and drug dealers, and I am unafraid. I work with ex-cons and gang members, so clearly my battle is intense. *But my purpose is no more special than anyone else's.*

Whatever your vision is, you will have to decide to do whatever it takes to get there. You will have to now be very clear on the price you are willing to pay for your vision. You may get motivated by my words, but motivation is not enough to execute and stay in action. Willpower alone will not sustain you. You will have to refuse to lose and become absolutely obsessed (despite what others say) with your vision coming to pass. The resistance will be too strong for you to be passive and still win. If you take any of this lightly, change won't come, not in its fullness.

You might not have the same heavy battles I have, but you are a warrior the same as I am, so you better get battle-ready. Women are warriors, (to call us only 'survivors' is offensive) and we are world-changers. We are *thrivers!* (Yes, that's a word, it means to grow strongly, vigorously, to do well and prosper)

Discipline will have to beat out procrastination. You will have to count the cost and train like there is no tomorrow. You will have to envision your obstacles, hit them at full speed and if you land on your ass some days, you gotta get back up. You will have to take extreme ownership over your dreams and get up every morning with the same fervency as you did the day before.

You cann*ot* have a *Plan B*. Burn your ships, remember? You have to create an environment where you won't settle, and you won't exit stage left. No Plan B means fulfilling your destiny is *your only option*. It's *that* serious. You know why? Because, without a vision, people perish. You die inside, and you find yourself at the end of your life, wishing you had lived more passionately.

Now It's Time

Now it's time to visualize a picture of what you want and who you are becoming. Picture what you want, build a scene in your mind detail-by-detail until you can see it...smell it...touch it. Faith utilizes our imagination, so anchor onto that picture in your mind by faith. Faith lets you see it in your heart before you see it in real life. It is the power of *believing* before seeing, the substance by which THAT scene will happen, THAT vision will be built and THAT dream will manifest into real life.

I visualized like this every step of the way. I dreamed my life in detail and then I manifested it into reality. How? I did it by *picturing my future,* then *writing it down*. After I wrote it down in a journal, I *made an action plan* to turn that dream into reality. *I scheduled my dreams and I calendared my victories.*

The reason you got this book is because, for you, the *Time* to prepare yourself, envision your life and start living out your purpose is *Now*. It is not a coincidence that you are reading *this,* at *this* point in your life, *right now.*

Finding and keeping our life mate is one of the most important decisions of our lives, second only to deciding to live our purpose. Who we partner with for the rest of our lives will be interconnected to every area of our lives. We cannot passively allow mediocrity, contempt, adultery, or irreconcilable differences to steal our marriage or hurt our children. We must go for the best to get it: the best marriage, and our best life.

Our unique purpose on this planet is ours to discover and fulfill, joyfully establishing our place in this world, making the best mark on it we can.

You get to *live out* the purpose you were made *on purpose* to do! You are never limited by your circumstances. You are already equipped for the journey.

IT'S TIME.

Envision it: your good man, your thriving marriage—*your best life*—is waiting for you.

Take a leap and don't look back.

Chapter 12

90-Day Challenge

We made it to this point! Together, as sisters. This is HUGE. You followed through, kept your commitment to read it all with an open mind. To make it to this point required some serious self-examination, so great job, girl! I mean it. Most people on the planet walk through life totally unaware, unwilling to do the hard work to change, so I am amazed by you and blessed to walk this process out with you.

Transforming ourselves is a never-ending process of growth throughout our lives, and that's a good thing! This book, this challenge, is only a first step on the journey to the best you. We never 'arrive', we just keep getting better...and that is what makes the journey exciting. We reach a milestone, we rest, reflect, enjoy it, and then we create and dream and get going again to our next destination. This is adventurous, set-your-soul-on-fire living! Being grateful for where we are, we build anticipation for our next big thing, and we don't apologize for wanting it. We don't allow others to limit us or transfer their attitudes and perceptions on to us, as it's never too late to be anything and everything we ever wanted to be.

Keep your mind clear of the 'I can't do this' kind of self-talk. Your body will follow what your brain tells it to, and your brain will follow what YOU tell it to. Tell yourself I can do this! I am worth it! It's good to want more out of my relationships, my parenting and my career! It's good to want millions of dollars to change my life and others'! It's good to hunger for success!

As you read and explore, you will find yourself wanting more and doing more, because you are expanding your learning capacity. That's how the brain works, so feed it. Pour in the good, breathe in the best, and then write down a plan of action; the first step to the top of the mountain. If you have to rest during your journey, go ahead, rest, but only for a minute. Don't let those muscles of success atrophy. Honor any discomfort of the soul as it heals and gets stronger, but keep moving. It's alright to feel weary at times because this process is not for the faint-of-heart, but you are reading this so you already on your way to being in the 2% of people that will fulfill their purpose!

Nothing is by accident and you didn't make it this far to just put this book down and go. You were made for more. This 90-Day Challenge is designed to rouse you to action, get you moving and to stoke the fire in that belly of yours. I am encouraging you and reminding you that you already have what it takes to face your fears, so just (by faith) tap into the limitless flow of courage and power God has put in you, and push past your current reality.

Give yourself permission to dream as big and as wild as you want. Let the visions in your head be filled with all that you desire for your future and then attach it to a mission. A mission is what you want now and how you will achieve your long-term dream, basically an action plan. Don't make your life be about the money. Make it about the mission and the money will follow. Figure out and do what you love, and you will never work a day in your life. That's when the miraculous doors open, the marriage falls in to place or the man of your dreams arrives and the life you once had stuck in your head begins to manifest before your eyes.

So. This 90-Day Challenge will be the first steps of your mission to transform your thinking, your body, your behaviors, your home and your relationships. Take each step seriously. And keep with me after the 90-Day Challenge, because I'll still be here, I'm in it for the long haul! I'll keep encouraging you to live more. My team will keep you inspired. You are not alone!

90-Day Challenge

Look at your calendar, and select the next 90 days, marking it somehow on your usual calendar so you can reference it daily. These next 25 steps will be fun, challenging and transforming! Read through the whole list first, then start with number 1. Here we go!

1. How Do You Feel? Write 2 pages:

Page 1) Did you have any strong responses to what you were reading? Did you feel angry, excited, irritated? Connect to the emotion and ask yourself: where or who do those feelings come from? Was there an event in your life that caused those feelings? Just pour out your heart about how you felt through the process of reading the book.

Page 2) How do you define or feel about femininity and masculinity?

2. Who Is Your Good Guy? Write 2 pages:

Page 1) What do you believe a good man is? How does he act and what does he do?

Page 2) Write another page on your dream man. What does he look like, how does he treat you? Do you have children together? What does he do for a living? What are his hobbies, his political views, his habits, his pace of life?

If you are married, how do you desire your husband to treat you or show up in the marriage? Dream...just pour it out on paper. Make a long list of the reasons you married him and compare it to this new list. Identify what you can build on but do not use this list to hold against him. This is just to identify what you want. Then we strategically use the tools I shared with you to create the relationship you desire.

3. Look In The Mirror and Get To Know Yourself

Look deep into your own eyes for at least 90 seconds. Introduce yourself to yourself. Declare change. Commit to doing what it takes to change. Promise to be kind to yourself through your transformation. Ask yourself for forgiveness for how you have treated yourself and commit to loving yourself more.

4. Get Feedback

Ask three women you trust to give you feedback about your character. Sit across from them, arms unfolded, open to hearing what they have to say. Ask them, how do you experience me? If you trust them, you should receive what they love about you and what behaviors are not serving you. Remember, it's only feedback designed for you to learn from. Feedback will not kill you, it will help you prepare for change.

5. Go Out To Lunch

Find three women you admire, women that have the career you might want, or are good mothers, or have style and elegance you aspire to have, or women who are simply 'solid', stable and on a mission. Ask them out to lunch (either all together or not). Pay for their lunch. Then ask them to be in your life, to any degree they are able to, without pressure. Explain you want to change your life and you admire them, you promise to not be needy or weird, you only want to connect with amazing women because you desire become a better woman.

6. Confess

Find one very trusted sister and confess your darkest secret to her...and let it go. Explain why: you are confessing because we are as sick as our secrets and that you want to be free, and leave it at that. You will feel uncomfortable at first, even for days, then free.

7. Clean Up The Hood

Grab some paper and give your closest friends a grade, from an A+ to an F, on their kindness, how they support your vision, how encouraging and forgiving they are, and if they are givers or takers. Then quietly and respectfully disengage from the D and F friends in your life. Intentionally invest in your A and B relationships, instead, getting to know those friends more intimately.

8. Refuse to Male-Bash for 90 Days

Do not speak negatively about men.

9. Write Your Obituary

If you were to die today, write your obituary, from your perspective, of the life you have lived up until this day. Did you contribute to the world? What kind of parent were you, or wife or friend? Did you fulfill your dreams or go after your passions?

10. Do You Love Your Body? Write 2 pages

Page 1) How do you relate to your physical body? How do you connect to it emotionally? How do you emotionally relate to your health, your size, your skin?

Page 2) What is your vision for your body, your weight, your health, endurance and overall well being? What are your goals and commitments to transform your body?

11. Get a Make-Up Makeover

Go to Benefit, MAC, Urban Decay or Sephora (or some department store) and get a make-up makeover. You only have to buy $30-$40 worth' of product for the makeover. Ask for tips on how to update your look, including making it age-appropriate.

12. Get a Hair Makeover

Go to a trendy salon (save your Starbucks money if you have to) and ask for a consultation. Be vulnerable. Ask if your look is dated and make a plan to get a new look, also age-appropriate.

13. Get a Style Makeover

Ask three women 10 years younger than you (if you are 30 and over) that are trendy, stylish and seem to have a good understanding about fashion, for their honest feedback on your style vibe, and then ask for their help to reinvent your look.

14. Burn Your Grandma Panties

Yes, actually burn all versions of your grandma panties. Wear sexy undies to bed that are comfortable. There are comfortable sexy panties, google them if u have to!

15. Compliment Your Man

Compliment your husband or the man you intend to marry, every single day. Sincerely acknowledge the good things he does, with genuine emotion. If you do not have a good man, practice on your father or a man you admire and respect and do it appropriately.

16. Sex

If you are single, no sex for 90 days. Tell the man you are with that you need his help and support and that you have decided to completely transform your life and you need time to do it. Ask respectfully, then listen carefully to how he responds, *it will be very revealing*. If you are married, initiate spicy fun sex at least once a week.

17. Smile At People

Everywhere you go, intentionally smile.

18. Give

Give something you love to someone at least once and don't explain why.

19. Keep Your Word

If you break a promise, acknowledge it and ask for forgiveness immediately.

20. Listen to One Positive Podcast Per Day

Every day for 90 days, listen to a motivating podcast or a You-Tube video. Every day of my life, I put my headphones on and listen to a motivating podcast. Depending on my mood and the day's mission, I choose between spiritual, motivational or self-help. TD Jakes, Joyce Meyer for spiritual, Jenna Kutcher with her Goal Digger podcast and Russell Brunson from Clickfunnels for business, 'Be Inspired' videos on YouTube, or Gary Vee, Tony Robbins, Brendon Burchard or Jordan Peterson for habits, motivation and success. Get your headphones on and pour in the good.

21. Take Account Every Night Before Sleep

Before you go to sleep, take an account. If you have broken a promise to someone or yourself, confess, ask for forgiveness and recommit.

22. Your Vision Board

For six days, take notes about your vision and gather pictures to put on a vision board for the seventh day. Gather your dream. Think it through. Mediate on it. On the seventh day, put the vision board together and write a two page letter to yourself about your vision, and put it on the board. Then make a list of the first 10 steps to take quick action on your dream. Execute these steps within 6 months or sooner.

23. Better Together

Find three women to read this book and do this 90-Day Challenge with. Even if they are behind you in reading the book, still connect with them during their process and commit to getting together at least two times a month.

24. Share

Ask three women to allow you to share your vision board and action plan with them and request they hold you accountable to that action plan.

25. Join the Always Be Hot Facebook Group

For daily inspiration, fun motivation and a growing sisterhood, sign up at **www.danabryant.com**

Made in the USA
Columbia, SC
31 January 2019